• T R O P H I E S •

Extra Support Copying Masters

Grade 2 ◆ Volumes 1 and 2

Harcourt

Orlando   Boston   Dallas   Chicago   San Diego

Visit *The Learning Site!*
www.harcourtschool.com

Printed in the United States of America

ISBN 0-15-323512-8

6 7 8 9 10 018 10 09 08 07 06 05 04

Contents

JUST FOR YOU

The Mixed-Up Chameleon. 1, 3–4, 6–9

Get Up and Go! 10, 12–13, 15–17

Henry and Mudge Under the Yellow Moon 18, 20–21, 23–25

Days With Frog and Toad. 26, 28–29, 31–33

Wilson Sat Alone. 34, 36–37, 39–41

The Enormous Turnip 42, 44–45, 47–50

Helping Out 51, 53–54, 56–58

Mr. Putter and Tabby Fly the Plane 59, 61–62, 64–66

Hedgehog Bakes a Cake 67, 69–70, 72–75

Lemonade for Sale. 76, 78–79, 81-84

Johnny Appleseed 85, 87–88, 90–92

From Seed to Plant 93, 95–96, 98–100

The Secret Life of Trees 101, 103–104, 106–108

Watermelon Day 109, 111–112, 114–116

Pumpkin Fiesta 117, 119–120, 122–124

Contents

BANNER DAYS

The Day Jimmy's Boa Ate the Wash. 1, 3–4, 6–9

How I Spent My Summer Vacation 10, 12–13, 15–17

Dear Mr. Blueberry. 18, 20–21, 23–25

Cool Ali. 26, 28–29, 31–33

The Emperor's Egg 34, 36–37, 39–41

The Pine Park Mystery. 42, 44–45, 47–50

Good-bye, Curtis 51, 53–54, 56–58

Max Found Two Sticks 59, 61–62, 64–66

Anthony Reynoso: Born to Rope 67, 69–70, 72–74

Chinatown. 75, 77–78, 80–82

Abuela 83, 85–86, 88–90

Beginner's World Atlas 91, 93–94, 96–98

Dinosaurs Travel 99, 101–102, 104–106

Montigue on the High Seas. 107, 109–110, 112–114

Ruth Law Thrills a Nation 115, 117–118, 120–122

· T R O P H I E S ·

Volume One

Just For You

Name _____

▶ **Circle and write the word that completes each sentence.**

1. The lizards _____ side by side.

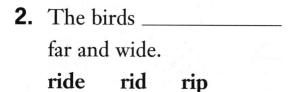

him   hide   hip

2. The birds _____
far and wide.

ride   rid   rip

3. The dogs _____
on the ice outside.

sky   slime   slide

4. The snake _____ under the lid.

hid   his   him

5. The rabbit tried to climb

_____ .

outside   inside   above

6. The river was too _____
to jump to the other side.

win   wide   with

SCHOOL-HOME CONNECTION With your child, think of action words with the letters –ide or –id. Ask your child to write sentences with some action words. Have him or her draw a picture that tells about the sentences.

1

Extra Support
Just for You

▶ **Read the word. Circle the pictures with names that have the same vowel sound and ending letters.**

1. hide

2. bid

3. pride

▶ **Read the sentences. Write the word that best completes each one.**

4. The lion opened its _____ mouth.
    wade   wide   white

5. The mother lamb looked for its _____.
                kid   kite   kiss

6. Your eyebrow is above your _____.
            ice cream   eyelid   eraser

SCHOOL-HOME CONNECTION Help your child to write a story about what it would be like to be a chameleon. Have your child use words with –ide and –id. Ask him or her to point out those words.

3

Extra Support
Just for You

▶ **Draw a line from each Vocabulary Word on the left to its meaning on the right.**

1. dull •   • to the left or to
                      the right

2. exciting •   • shining or glittering

3. handsome •   • saw

4. hardly •   • very interesting

5. sideways •   • almost not

6. sparkling •   • not shiny

7. spotted •   • very good-looking

 TRY THIS! Write three sentences about a trip to the zoo. Use as many Vocabulary Words as possible. Draw a picture of something you write about.

Extra Support
Just for You

Name _____

▶ **Write the number of syllables you hear in each picture name.**

coat

bicycle

lizard

1. _____

2. _____

3. _____

baseball

target

snake

4. _____

5. _____

6. _____

winter

sleeping

grasshopper

7. _____

8. _____

9. _____

Extra Support
Just for You

Name _____

▶ **Read the paragraph. Then choose the best answer to each question. Fill in the circle next to your choice.**

Friday's Trip

Ana's class will go to the zoo. The trip is planned for Friday. Ana will visit the monkey house. She also hopes to see the seals. Ana likes teddy bears. She can't wait until Friday.

1 What is the main idea of the paragraph?

○ Ana likes to see the elephants.

○ Ana will see seals at the zoo.

○ Ana's class will go to the zoo.

○ Ana has never been to a zoo.

Tip

Reread the first sentence of the paragraph. The first sentence is often the main idea.

2 Which sentence does not belong in the paragraph?

○ Ana will visit the monkey house.

○ Ana likes teddy bears.

○ The trip is planned for Friday.

○ She can't wait until Friday.

Tip

Try reading the paragraph without each answer choice.

SCHOOL-HOME CONNECTION With your child, read a favorite story. Ask your child what he or she thinks is the main idea of the story.

7

Extra Support
Just for You

Name _____

▶ **Look at the Table of Contents page. Then answer the questions.**

Chapter One	Red Fox	*page 1*
Chapter Two	White Bear	*page 5*
Chapter Three	Yellow Giraffe	*page 10*
Chapter Four	Gray Elephant	*page 15*

1 What is the name of Chapter One?

○ Animals of All Colors

○ Table of Contents

○ Red Fox

> 💡 **Tip**
> Read the names of each chapter.

2 Which chapter is about yellow giraffe?

○ Chapter One

○ Chapter Two

○ Chapter Three

> 💡 **Tip**
> Look at the name of each chapter. Look at the number of each chapter.

3 Which page does Chapter Four start on?

○ page 5

○ page 10

○ page 15

SCHOOL-HOME CONNECTION With your child, look through a book with a table of contents. Show your child how to find the various chapters.

8

Extra Support
Just for You

Name _____

▶ **Write the words from the box that best complete the poem. Remember that the word you write should rhyme with the last word in the line above.**

| did | ride | slide | inside |

One day a lizard tried to hide.

Under a leaf it tried to _____.

But the leaf wasn't that wide.

A hole! The lizard went _____.

The lizard slept. The lizard hid.

And the next thing that the lizard _____.

Was poke his little head outside.

Look a friend! Let's take a _____!

SCHOOL-HOME CONNECTION Talk with your child about rhyming words with –ide and –id endings, such as *hid, lid, bid* or *hide, slide, wide*. Ask him or her to choose two of each type that rhyme. Make a poem card by folding a sheet of paper in half. Encourage your child to write a short poem using these words on the inside of the card. Have your child draw a picture telling about the poem on the outside of the card.

Extra Support
Just for You

▶ **Write the letters needed to complete each picture name.**

1. _____ sn _ k _____

2. _____ n _ m _____

3. _____ s _ m _____

4. _____ m _ k _____

5. _ mist _ k _____

6. _____ br _ k _____

7. _ fl _ m _____

8. _ g _ m _ s _____

SCHOOL-HOME CONNECTION Invite your child to draw pictures of things he or she does each morning. Help your child write a caption for the pictures that include the phonics words.

10

Extra Support
Just for You

▶ **Write the word that makes each sentence tell about the picture.**

| take | name | make | games | snake | same |

1. Kate does the _____ things every morning.

2. Kate plays _____ with her dog.

3. Her dog's _____ is Max.

4. Max can _____ Kate late for school.

5. Kate also has a _____.

6. Today Kate will _____ her snake to school.

SCHOOL-HOME CONNECTION Look around your home for ways to use phonics words. For example, a full trash can might be, "*Take* out the trash." Cooking dinner could be, "We *make* dinner." Have your child repeat the sentences, stressing the phonics words.

12

Extra Support
Just for You

► **Complete each sentence with a Vocabulary Word from the box.**

| always | homework | minutes | snuggle | treat |

1. The work I do at home is called

   _____.

2. There are sixty _____ in every hour.

3. Popcorn is my favorite _____ after school.

4. I _____ brush my teeth before bedtime.

5. My cat Puff likes to cuddle and

   _____ near our dog.

TRY THIS! Write a few sentences about a pet. Use as many Vocabulary Words as you can in your story.

Extra Support
Just for You

Name _____

▶ **Find the word that has the same sound as the underlined letters in the first word.**

Example: b<u>ake</u>

    ○ name

    ○ bike

    ● lake

1 n<u>ame</u>

    ○ take

    ○ lamb

    ○ same

> **Tip**
> Sound out each answers choice yourself.

2 g<u>ame</u>

    ○ shame

    ○ rake

    ○ page

3 r<u>ake</u>

    ○ arm

    ○ snake

    ○ ram

> **Tip**
> Skip any choices that don't make sense.

4 l<u>ake</u>

    ○ bark

    ○ chart

    ○ wake

Extra Support
Just for You

Name _____

▶ **Read the signs. Then answer each question.**
Write your answer on the line.

BE ON TIME FOR SCHOOL!
You have to be in school by 8:30 in the morning.
That's when all classes start! Here's how to be on time.
Get your clothes ready the night before. Wake up early.
Have a good breakfast. Get to the bus stop ten
minutes before the bus comes.

The author is telling you _____

What was the author's purpose for writing this sign?
(Hint: Authors have different reasons for writing.)

_____

SCOTT FOR BEST CLOWN
Vote for Scott! He is the funniest clown in the
circus. He will make you laugh.

What was the author's purpose for writing this sign?

_____

_____

SCHOOL-HOME CONNECTION Look at a few
types of writing with your child, such as recipes,
instructions and advertisements. Ask your child
why the author wrote each type.

16

Extra Support
Just for You

Name _____

▶ **Read the sentences. Circle the words that contain the letters *id* or *ide*.**

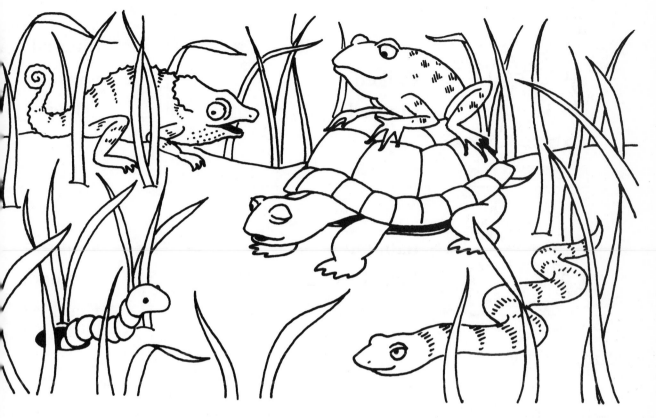

1. A chameleon can hide in the grass.

2. A snake can slide through the grass.

3. A frog can ride on a turtle.

4. A turtle can close one eyelid.

5. A worm is inside a hole in the grass.

SCHOOL-HOME CONNECTION Look through magazines or picturebooks with your child. Point out items that sound like the phonics words, such as *wide, inside, ride, hide, hid, kid,* and *ride.* Invite your child to point out ideas, too.

17

Extra Support
Just for You

Name _____

▶ **Choose the word that goes with the picture.**
Write the word on the line.

1.

barked
walked
jumped

_____

2.

opened
wished
asked

_____

3.

napped
licked
leaped

4.

shouted
yawned
thanked

5.

talked
helped
painted

6.

backed
barked
picked

_____

7.

marked
mailed
melted

8.

jumped
chilled
checked

_____

SCHOOL-HOME CONNECTION Invite your child
to choose a word, draw a picture to illustrate it
and then label it. Have your child cover up the
label and ask you to guess the word.

18

Extra Support
Just for You

► **On each line, write the word from the box that makes the most sense.**

checked	remarked	thanked
barked	licked	opened

1. "My dog is missing,"

Ben _____.

2. Ben _____
the closet.

3. Ben _____
under the bed.

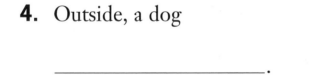
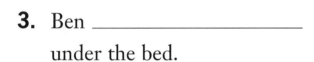

4. Outside, a dog

_____.

5. Ben _____
Jill.

6. Ben's dog _____
his face.

SCHOOL-HOME CONNECTION Talk about the
words with your child. Ask your child to act out
each word to show what it means.

20

Extra Support
Just for You

▶ **Write a Vocabulary Word from the box to complete each unfinished sentence.**

chipmunks	picked	sniffing	south	woods

1. People live in towns and cities. Rabbits

   live in the ———————————.

2. The dog smells the meat. He starts

   ——————————— the bag.

3. Fish swim in water. Most ———————————

   climb trees.

4. First, we saw some apple trees. Then we

   ——————————— some apples.

5. Birds fly north in the spring. Birds fly

   ——————————— in the fall.

 TRY THIS! Write two or three sentences about what you like to do in the fall. Use as many Vocabulary Words as you can.

Extra Support
Just for You

Name _____

▶ **Find the word in which the letters *ed* have the same sound they have in the first word.**

Example: paint<u>ed</u>

   ○ backed

   ○ yelled

   ● drifted

1 wait<u>ed</u>

   ○ sailed

   ○ shouted

   ○ missed

> **Tip**
> Look at the underlined letters. Listen for the sound they make when you sound out the word.

2 bark<u>ed</u>

   ○ touched

   ○ landed

   ○ dusted

3 aim<u>ed</u>

   ○ crossed

   ○ sifted

   ○ spotted

Extra Support
Just for You

Name _____

▶ **Read the paragraph. Then choose the best answer to each question. Circle your answer.**

Sam's Days

Sam always has a great time with his grandma and grandpa. He stays with them every August. Each morning he takes a long walk with their dog, Blue. On his walk he says hello to the horses in the barn. Then he watches Grandpa feed the pigs. Sam says, "I like the pigs the best."

1 Where is Sam?

on a farm

in a city

in a school

at a playground

2 When does the story take place?

in the winter

in the fall

in the summer

in the spring

SCHOOL-HOME CONNECTION With your child, retell a fairy tale or folktale you both enjoy. Ask your child where the story is set. Discuss whether the setting changes.

24

Extra Support
Just for You

Name _____

Henry and Mudge
Under the Yellow
Moon
Review:

Phonograms:
-ame, -ake

▶ **Read the story. Circle all the words with the letters *ame* or *ake*. Write each word in the chart.**

One day, Jason saw a snake. He took the snake home. He gave the snake a name. He played games with the snake. He tried to make the snake happy, but the snake became sad. Jason had made a mistake. He had to take the snake back. "Good-bye," said Jason. The snake was happiest in the grass.

1.	
2.	
3.	
4.	
5.	
6.	
7.	

SCHOOL-HOME CONNECTION Talk with your child about why the snake might have become sad. What might the snake have missed? Have your child draw a picture of a happy snake in the grass and the things it enjoys. Have your child label the things in the picture.

25

Name _____

▶ **Write the letters *ied* or *ed* to complete each picture name.**

1. stud _____

2. ___ cr _____

3. ___ carr _____

4. check _____

5. cop _____

6. call _____

7. hurr _____

8. walk _____

9. jump _____

10. boil _____

11. fr _____

12. marr _____

SCHOOL-HOME CONNECTION Ask your child
to point to each phonics word that ends by
changing the *y* to *-ied*. Take turns saying each
word with the *y* ending, then with the *-ied* ending.

 26

Extra Support
Just for You

Name _____

▶ **Read the word. Circle the pictures whose names have the same vowel sounds.**

1. carried

2. tried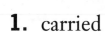

3. replied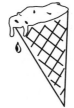

▶ **Read the sentences. Write the word that best completes each one.**

4. I _____ for the test.

　　stoked　　studied　　stained

5. I _____ home from school.

　　hurried　　hardened　　hinted

6. I _____ my spelling words.

　　coped　　cupped　　copied

SCHOOL-HOME CONNECTION Make up new sentences with your child, using the phonics words. Encourage your child to choose a favorite sentence to illustrate.

28

Extra Support
Just for You

Name _____

▶ **Draw a line from each Vocabulary Word on the left to its meaning on the right.**

1. alone　　•

•　to make happy

2. cheer　　•

•　ruined

3. fine　　•

•　very good

4. meadow　•

•　why something happens

5. reason　•

•　by yourself

6. spoiled　•

•　a field

 TRY THIS! Choose a Vocabulary Word. On a separate sheet of paper, draw a picture to show its meaning. Below the drawing, write a sentence using the Vocabulary Word.

Extra Support
Just for You

Name _____

Skill Reminder • **Divide a word between the base word and the ending.**

▶ Read each word. Then add an *ed* ending to the word. Write the new two syllable word.

Base word	Base Word + Ending
act	1. _____
toast	2. _____
blend	3. _____
hunt	4. _____
fold	5. _____

▶ Read each word. Write the number of syllables in each word. Write the syllables.

Word List	Number of Syllables
boasted	6. _____
carried	7. _____
cried	8. _____
mended	9. _____
tried	10. _____

Extra Support
Just for You

Name _____

HOMEWORK

Days With Frog
and Toad

Compare and
Contrast
TEST PREP

▶ **Read the paragraph. Then choose the best answer to each question. Fill in the circle next to your choice.**

Zeke the zebra and Snappy the snail are friends. They both like being outside. Zeke is a fast runner, but Snappy is slow. Zeke likes carrots. Snappy likes apples. Zeke likes to play. Snappy hides under a rock. "Snappy is not like me, but we are still friends," says Zeke. Zeke does all the talking. Snappy is the quiet one.

1 What is the same about Zeke and Snappy?

- ○ Zeke is a zebra.
- ○ Snappy moves slowly.
- ○ They both talk a lot.
- ○ They both like being outside.

💡 **Tip**

Read the paragraph to check each answer choice. Look for the word *both*. What do both Zeke and Snappy like to do?

2 What is different about Zeke and Snappy?

- ○ Zeke and Snappy like to eat.
- ○ Snappy and Zeke are animals.
- ○ Zeke is fast and Snappy is slow.
- ○ Snappy and Zeke are friends.

💡 **Tip**

Read the paragraph to check each answer choice. Look for the word *but*.

SCHOOL-HOME CONNECTION With your child, compare and contrast some simple items in your kitchen. For example, have your child find items that are alike because they come in boxes. Then contrast the contents of the boxes.

Extra Support
Just for You

Name _____

Days with Frog
and Toad

Review:
Inflections Word
ending: *-ed*

▶ **Read the story. Circle all the words that end
with *ed*. Write the words on the chart.**

One day, Stacey got a letter. It was from

Uncle Lou. It had exciting news! Stacey

painted a picture of the news. She mailed it

to Uncle Lou. A few weeks later, Uncle Lou

came to visit. He backed his car into the drive. He opened the door. Out

came a puppy! The puppy barked and licked Stacey's hand. Stacey thanked

her Uncle Lou. "He's the best dog!" she remarked.

1.	
2.	
3.	
4.	
5.	
6.	
7.	
8.	

SCHOOL-HOME CONNECTION Ask your child
how he or she would react to getting a new pet.
Have your child paint the pet's picture and write a
sentence using words that end in *ed*.

33

Extra Support
Just for You

Name _____

▶ **Choose the word with *at* or *ate* that names the picture. Write the word on the line.**

1.

goat
gate
got

_____

2.

act
acorn
acrobat

_____

3.

cat
cape
car

_____

4.

plate
pad
plug

_____

5.

site
shore
state

_____

6.

crown
create
cream

_____

7.

sat
salt
sang

_____

8.

appreciate
appear
apparel

_____

SCHOOL-HOME CONNECTION Act out several of the phonics words, asking your child to guess the word. Then have your child illustrate one of the words and label it.

34

Extra Support
Just for You

Name _____

▶ **Read the word. Circle the pictures whose names have the same sound as the underlined word.**

1. <u>that</u>

2. <u>ate</u>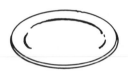

3. <u>late</u>

▶ **Read the sentences. Write the word that best completes each one.**

4. The bubbly soda went _____.

              fly   **flat**   **flake**

5. We can _____ a new painting.

    crease   **crane**   **create**

6. The _____ flipped across the floor.

    acrobat   **accent**   **acorn**

SCHOOL-HOME CONNECTION Write each phonics word on a card or slip of paper. Say the words. Ask your child to listen for *at* or *ate*. Have your child sort the word cards into separate piles for the two sounds.

36

Extra Support
Just for You

▶ **Circle the correct answer. Then write the Vocabulary Word on the line.**

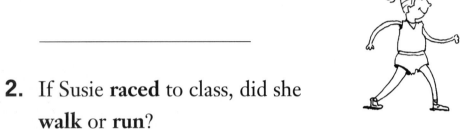

| amazing | clustered | gathered | raced | wandered |

1. If your dad **gathered** leaves, did he make
   a pile or **a fire**?

   _____

2. If Susie **raced** to class, did she
   walk or **run**?

   _____

3. If the kids **clustered** around the truck, were they
   together or **apart**?

   _____

4. If Stanley **wandered** through the store, did he walk
   fast or **slow**?

   _____

5. If the ball game was **amazing**, was it

   interesting or **boring**? _____

 TRY THIS! Write a few sentences about a winter activity you enjoy. Use as many Vocabulary Words as you can in your sentences.

Extra Support
Just for You

Name _____

| **Syllable Rule** | Divide a compound word between |

the two smaller words in it.

Example: hot/dog sail/boat

▶ **Read the sentence. The compound word is underlined.
Write the word in syllables.**

1. The news <u>broadcast</u> was
shown all over the country.

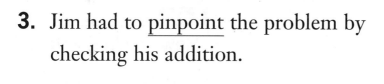

   broad / cast

2. <u>Bookstores</u> have lots of books for
people to buy.

_____

3. Jim had to <u>pinpoint</u> the problem by
checking his addition.

_____

4. Ann did not hear what I said because
she had a <u>daydream</u>.

_____

5. My dog sleeps in a <u>doghouse</u>.

_____

Name _____

▶ **Read the paragraph. Then choose the best answer to each question. Fill in the circle next to your choice.**

Marla Reads

Marla stood at the front of the classroom. Her hands were shaking. She had never read a story to her classmates before. Her voice shook at first. Then Marla's words became louder and clearer. At the end, the whole class clapped. Marla took a bow and smiled. Reading aloud was fun!

1 How does Marla feel at the beginning of the story?

○ sad   ○ tired

○ nervous   ○ bored

> **Tip**
> How would you feel if your hands were shaking?

2 How does Marla feel at the end of the story?

○ annoyed   ○ unhappy

○ upset   ○ proud

> **Tip**
> How would you feel if people were clapping for you?

3 Where does Marla read the story?

○ in the classroom

○ on the playground

○ in the office

○ in the hall

> **Tip**
> The setting is often found in the beginning. Try reading the first few sentences again.

SCHOOL-HOME CONNECTION With your child, talk about a time when he or she tried something new. Then invite your child to write a sentence and draw a picture illustrating his or her experience.

40

Extra Support
Just for You

Name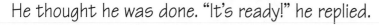

▶ **Read the story. Circle all the words that end with *–ed*. Write the words on the chart.**

The cook studied the recipe. He fried some

bacon and eggs. He cried as he cut the onions.

He tried to mix the batter. He made a mess!

Then he hurried. He worried dinner would be late.

He thought he was done. "It's ready!" he replied.

He carried the dish to the table. He fell! What a mess!

1.	
2.	
3.	
4.	
5.	
6.	
7.	
8.	

SCHOOL-HOME CONNECTION Ask your child to draw a picture of the story character after dropping the food. Help your child write a few sentences about the picture, using the phonics words.

Extra Support
Just for You

▶ **Write the letters *ack* or *ock* to complete each picture name. Then trace the whole word.**

1. cl _____

2. p _____

3. r _____ et

4. cr _____

5. fl _____

6. l _____

7. horseb _____

8. d _____

9. sn _____

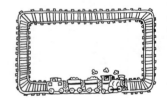

10. bl _____

11. sh _____

12. tr _____

Extra Support
Just for You

▶ **The word at the top and the picture names in each row should rhyme. Write the picture names. Then write another rhyming word and draw a picture for it.**

black

1. _____ _____ _____

shock

2. _____ _____ _____

socket

3. _____ _____ _____

Extra Support
Just for You

Name _____

▶ **On each line, write a Vocabulary Word from
the box to complete the sentence.**

| enormous | granddaughter | grew | planted | strong | turnip |

1. The daughter of one's son or daughter is called a

   _____ .

2. If your plant got bigger, it _____
   taller.

3. If something is very large, it is

   _____ .

4. A seed is _____
   in the ground.

5. A _____
   is a kind of vegetable.

6. If you lift a stack of books, you need to be

   _____ .

TRY THIS! Pick two words from the box above. Write one sentence using both words. Draw a picture for your sentence.

Name _____

Syllable Rule • **When two consonants that are the same come between two vowels in a word, divide between the consonants:** *bot / tle.*

▶ Read the words. Divide them into syllables using a slash mark (/).

arrow   1. _____

barrel   2. _____

bottom   3. _____

comma   4. _____

follow   5. _____

happen   6. _____

mirror   7. _____

pizza   8. _____

traffic   9. _____

yellow   10. _____

Extra Support
Just for You

Name _____

▶ **Read the paragraph. Then choose the best answer to each question. Fill in the circle next to your choice.**

Mei's Tomatoes

Every year, Mei grows tomatoes. First, she buys seeds. She puts the seeds in the soil. Then Mei waters the soil every day. The seeds grow into big red tomatoes. Mei waits until they are ripe. Finally, Mei picks them and gives them to her neighbors.

1 The first thing Mei does is

○ buy seeds.

○ put the seeds in soil.

○ water the soil.

○ give the tomatoes to her neighbors.

> **Tip**
> In the paragraph, find the sentence with the word *first*.

2 The last thing Mei does is

○ water the soil.

○ put the seeds in soil.

○ give the tomatoes away.

○ wait until they are ripe.

> **Tip**
> In the paragraph, find the sentence with the word *finally*.

SCHOOL-HOME CONNECTION With your child, look through a recipe for a favorite food. Talk about the sequence of the steps. Then invite your child to point out the first and last steps in the recipe.

48

Extra Support
Just for You

▶ **Write the words in alphabetical order on the lines.**

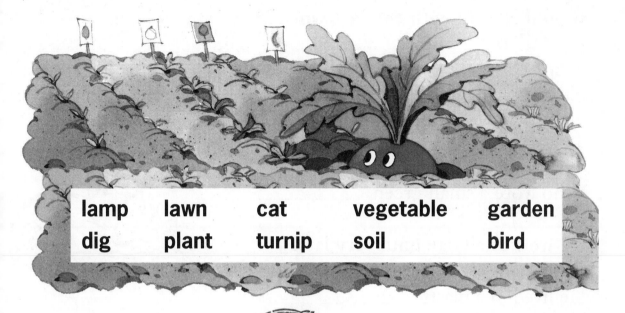

lamp	lawn	cat	vegetable	garden
dig	plant	turnip	soil	bird

1. bird

2. _____

3. dig

4. _____

5. lawn

6. _____

7. plant

8. _____

9. turnip

10. _____

 SCHOOL-HOME CONNECTION Help your child
write down the names of some classmates or
friends. Then assist your child in putting the
names in alphabetical order.

 49

▶ **Write the word that best completes each line of the poem. Remember that the word you write should rhyme with the last word in the line above.**

crate	hat	skate	fat

There was once a little gray cat

Who wore a small green _____.

He worked all day until very late.

He lived in a plastic _____.

He liked pancakes that were round and flat.

He liked them so much, he became

very _____.

The cat got sick from how much he ate.

He stopped eating. He learned how

to _____.

SCHOOL-HOME CONNECTION Say these words with your child: *appreciate* and *acrobat*. Encourage your child to think of ways to add them to the poem. For example, "The cat would appreciate some help. An acrobat joins the cat."

Extra Support
Just for You

▶ **Write the letters *ear* to complete each picture
name that has the *words*.**

1. _____th

2. __p____

3. _____n

4. __p__l__

5. __l__n__

6. __s__ch__

7. __h__t__

8. _____ly__

9. reh____se

SCHOOL-HOME CONNECTION Encourage your
child to come up with a sentence for each of the
words with the letters *ear*. Let your child illustrate
one sentence, and then write the sentence below
for a caption.

Extra Support
Just for You

Name _____

▶ **Write the word from the box that completes each sentence.**

rehearsed	early	learned
yearned	researched	heard

1. I _____ about auditions for the school play.

2. I _____ to be in the school play.

3. I _____ the roles.

4. I woke up

_____ .

5. I _____ my lines.

6. I _____ with the other actors.

Extra Support
Just for You

Name _____

► **Draw a line from each Vocabulary Word on the left to its meaning on the right.**

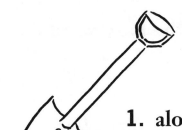

1. alongside •

• a machine that makes a car move

2. chores •

• to start to grow

3. engine •

• next to

4. simple •

• something you use when you work

5. sprout •

• jobs to do

6. tool •

• not hard to do

TRY THIS! Draw a picture of yourself helping someone. Then write about your picture. Use as many Vocabulary Words as you can.

54

Syllable Rule   Divide a two-syllable word ending in *-ing* or *-ly* between the base word and the ending.

• Divide a word that ends in *-ed* before the base word if the base word ends in *t* or *d*.

Examples:

| clear / ly | chew / ing | plant / ed |
| lone / ly | turn / ing | braid / ed |

▶ Divide the words into syllables. The first two have been done for you.

| burning | counted | singing | jumping | mashing |
| nearly | beaded | nicely | smoothly | waited |

1. burn / ing   2. count / ed

3. _____   4. _____

5. _____   6. _____

7. _____   8. _____

9. _____   10. _____

Extra Support
Just for You

Name _____

▶ **Read the paragraph. Then choose the best answer to each question. Fill in the circle next to your choice.**

Animal Tools

Some animals use tools to help them with their daily activities. The tools can help animals find food. Sea otters use rocks to smash shells so they can eat the meat inside. Otters like to float on their backs. Other animals use parts of their bodies as tools. The beaver uses its tail to build its home. It scoops mud onto its tail and then pats the mud between the logs.

1. What is the main idea of the paragraph?

○ Sea otters smash rocks.

○ Beavers scoop mud onto their tails.

○ Some animals use tools to help them.

○ Otters like to float on their backs.

 Tip
Reread the first sentence of the paragraph. The first sentence is often the main idea.

2. Which sentence does not belong in the paragraph?

○ The tools can help animals find food.

○ Otters like to float on their backs.

○ The beaver uses its tail to help build its home.

○ Other animals use parts of their bodies as tools.

 Tip
Try reading the paragraph without each answer choice.

SCHOOL-HOME CONNECTION Ask your child to read aloud a paragraph from a nonfiction children's book or magazine article. Then have your child tell you the main idea.

57

Extra Support
Just for You

Name _____

► **Write the words from the box that best
complete the poem. Remember that the word
you write should rhyme with the last word in the line above.**

crack	flock	rocket	horseback

Across my back I slung my pack.

Then I traveled on _____.

I was eating a small snack,

When suddenly I heard a _____.

My hands were still inside my pocket,

When the horse took off like a _____.

You should have seen my look of shock,

When we ran into the goose _____.

SCHOOL-HOME CONNECTION Help your child
to choose a moment from the poem to illustrate.
Have your child copy the corresponding lines from
the poem below the illustrations.

58

Extra Support
Just for You

Name _____

Mr. Putter and
Tabby Fly
the Plane

Common
Abbreviations

▶ **Look at the underlined word. Circle the abbreviation for the underlined word.**

1. <u>Doctor</u> Thompson is an animal doctor.　　**Dr.**　　**Mr.**　　**Mrs.**

2. The office is on Main <u>Street</u>.　　**Mr.**　　**St.**　　**Aug.**

3. Lee's cat had kittens in <u>August</u>.　　**Aug.**　　**Tues**　　**Mr.**

4. On <u>Wednesday</u>, Lee played with the kittens.　　**Sun.**　　**Jan.**　　**Wed.**

5. <u>Mister</u> Chen made a bed for the kittens.　　**Dr.**　　**Mr.**　　**Dec**

SCHOOL-HOME CONNECTION Have your child
draw pictures of people he or she knows. Help
your child label each picture with the person's
name and the correct abbreviation—*Mr., Mrs.,*
or *Dr.*

59

Extra Support
Just for You

Name _____

▶ **Write the abbreviation that completes
each sentence.**

Mr.	St.	Mrs.	Tues.	Jan.	Dr.

1. Mr. and _____ Brown's
dog, Freddy, was not feeling well.

2. Freddy's last check up

was in _____.

3. On _____, they
called the doctor.

4. _____ Cassidy said,
"Come to the office."

5. The doctor's office is

on Elm _____.

6. "Thank you, Dr. Cassidy,"

said _____ Brown.

SCHOOL-HOME CONNECTION With your child,
write a weekly schedule. For the days of the week,
use the abbreviations: *Sun., Tues., Wed.* Challenge
your child to abbreviate the remaining days: *Mon.,
Thurs., Fri., Sat.*

Extra Support
Just for You

▶ **Write a Vocabulary Word from the box to complete each unfinished sentence.**

cranes	directions	promise	twitch	worry

1. You make a _____
that you will play ball on Monday.

2. This book gives _____
to make a boat.

3. Workers move large, heavy things

with _____ .

4. Does your nose _____
when it itches ?

5. You _____
when you lose your favorite toy car.

TRY THIS! Draw a picture of your favorite toy. Then write three sentences telling why it is your favorite. Use as many Vocabulary Words as you can.

Name _____

Mr. Putter and
Tabby Fly
the Plane

Common
Abbreviations
TEST PREP

▶ **Choose the correct abbreviation for each word.**

Example: Mister

    ○ Mr

    ● Mr.

    ○ mr

1 Road

    ○ Rd.

    ○ rd

    ○ Rd

> 💡 **Tip**
> Most abbreviations start with a capital letter and end with a period.

2 Wednesday

    ○ Wd

    ○ wed.

    ○ Wed.

> 💡 **Tip**
> Abbreviations of days and months use the first few letters of the word.

3 Inch

    ○ in

    ○ In.

    ○ in.

> 💡 **Tip**
> An abbreviation for a measurement doesn't usually start with a capital letter.

Extra Support
Just for You

Name _____

▶ **Read the story beginning. Think about what will happen next. Then write the correct answer on the line.**

Mrs. Tiny always wanted to fly in a balloon. "I want to see my house from the sky," she said. One day a circus came to town. There were clowns and elephants. There was also a balloon ride. The next day, Mrs. Tiny got up very early. She put on her flying clothes. She tucked her hair into a flying cap. "Now, I'm ready," she told herself.

1 What will Mrs. Tiny do next? ———

_____

_____

_____

> **Tip**
> Reread the first paragraph. How does Mrs. Tiny want to fly?

2 Will Mrs. Tiny fly in a balloon? ———

_____

3 What clue tells you what might happen?

_____

_____

> **Tip**
> Reread the paragraph. Look for clues about planning to fly in a balloon.

SCHOOL-HOME CONNECTION Read to your child the first part of a story he or she has never read. Invite your child to help you predict how it might end. Talk with your child about clues in the story that helped him or her predict.

Extra Support
Just for You

Name _____

Mr. Putter and
Tabby Fly
the Plane

Review:
R-controlled
vowels: /û/ear

▶ **Read the story. Circle all the words with *ear* that have the sound like *pearl*. Write all the words on the chart.**

There was once a little silk worm that yearned to fly. He heard that flying was even more fun than crawling through apples. So he did some research on the Worm-net on flying. He learned that you need wings to fly. He needed lots of silk to make his wings. He earned money doing chores around the hole to buy his supplies. Every night, he studied wing-making at his dirt desk. He rehearsed flying in an empty tunnel. After weeks of hard work, he finished his wings and went flying.

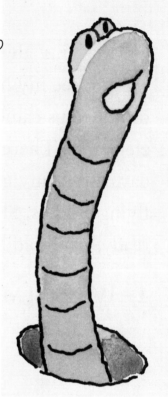

1.	
2.	
3.	
4.	
5.	
6.	

SCHOOL-HOME CONNECTION With your child, think of another animal that might want to experience something new. Ask your child to draw a picture of the animal, then to write a few sentences to tell about the animal, using the phonics words.

Extra Support
Just for You

Name _____

▶ **Look at the picture. Circle and write the word
that completes each sentence.**

1.	Marta picked _____ apples.	four for fore
2.	James likes to practice on the basketball _____.	corn core court
3.	She _____ a glass of milk for me.	poor poured pout
4.	I will practice hard so I can run the whole _____.	course cow couch
5.	There are _____ children in my class.	fourteen forth fourth

SCHOOL-HOME CONNECTION Look through some of your child's favorite books for words that contain *our*. Ask your child to read those words.

67

Extra Support
Just for You

Name _____

▶ **Read the sentences. Write the word that best completes each one.**

1. My sister is in _____ grade.

      fourth   form   four

2. A dictionary is a _____.

      resort   resource   recount

3. The number before five is _____.

      fort   far   four

4. People _____ when they are very sad.

      more   mourn   morning

5. What is the _____ of that noise?

      source   sore   sour

6. He _____ a big glass of juice.

      pout   poured   pop

SCHOOL-HOME CONNECTION Write each of the answer words from this lesson twice on separate slips of paper or index cards. Place all the cards face down. Ask your child to choose two cards. If they match, set the cards aside. Continue until all words are matched.

Extra Support
Just for You

Name _____

▶ **Read the first sentence in each pair. It gives you a clue. Write a Vocabulary Word from the box to complete each unfinished sentence.**

batter	buttery	perfect
recipe	smeared	yellow cake

1. How did you make that yummy cake? To find out how

to make cake, I read a _____.

2. I mixed butter, eggs, flour, and sugar.

I stirred the _____.

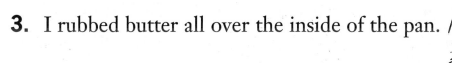

3. I rubbed butter all over the inside of the pan.

I _____ the butter.

4. The inside of the pan was covered with butter.

It was _____.

5. I baked the batter.

I made a _____.

6. The cake was just right. It was _____.

TRY THIS!
Make up a recipe for your favorite food. Write your recipe on
a sheet of paper. Use as many Vocabulary Words as you can.

Name _____

Syllable Rule	• **When two consonants come between two vowels in a word, divide after the first consonant.**

Example: pen/cil

• **When a two-syllable word with the VCCV pattern ends with s, es, or ed, the word is still divided after the first consonant.**

Example: thun/dered

▶ Say the words in each square to yourself. Write each word with the two endings. Listen to the number of syllables you hear. Then divide the word into syllables.

hammers s ed	question s ed
1. _____	3. _____
2. _____	4. _____
button s ed	wonder s ed
5. _____	7. _____
6. _____	8. _____

▶ **Read the questions. Choose the answer that fits best. Fill in the circle next to your choice.**

1. Which word is a synonym for alike?

○ different

○ same

○ funny

○ about

> **Tip**
> Synonyms are words with the same meaning. Look for a word that means the same as alike.

2 Which word does not mean the same as small?

○ little

○ tiny

○ petite

○ big

> **Tip**
> Make sure you read each question carefully. If you miss the word *not*, you may mark the wrong answer.

3 Which word is a synonym for noisy?

○ quiet

○ whisper

○ loud

○ soft

> **Tip**
> Sometimes more than one answer seems like it would fit best. Reread the question and choose the one that makes the most sense.

SCHOOL-HOME CONNECTION With your child, make a list of synonyms. Help your child use the synonyms in sentences.

73

Extra Support
Just for You

Name _____

▶ **Read the recipe. Then answer the questions.**

Directions

Things You Need

2 slices of bread

1 stick of butter

1 jar of honey

plastic knife

paper plate

1. First, wash your hands.
2. With the plastic knife cut a small piece of butter. Spread it on the bread.
3. Wash the knife in warm water.
4. Scoop a little honey from the jar with the knife. Spread it on the bread.
5. Put the slices of bread together.
6. Last, eat the sandwich. Yum!

HONEY

1 What do you need to make the sandwich?

○ salt, eggs, bread, knife

○ bread, jam, plate

○ bread, butter, honey, knife, plate

💡 **Tip**

You always need to make sure you have everything you need before you start. Read through the directions. Look for the list of the things you need.

2 What is the first thing you should do?

○ Wash the knife.

○ Wash your hands.

○ Spread honey on the bread.

💡 **Tip**

Following directions means following the steps in order. Watch for words like *first*. Also, pay attention to the number next to each step.

SCHOOL-HOME CONNECTION With your child prepare a dish following a recipe. Have your child help you by gathering up ingredients and measuring them out. Help your child read the recipe.

74

Extra Support
Just for You

Name _____

Hedgehog Bakes
a Cake

Review:
Common
Abbreviations

▶ **Read the words below. Write the abbreviation from the box beside the longer form of the word.**

Mr.	St.	Sun.	Dec.	Jan.
Dr.	Aug.	Tues.	Wed.	

1. doctor _____

2. street _____

3. Tuesday _____

4. August _____

5. Sunday _____

6. December _____

7. January _____

8. Wednesday _____

9. Mister _____

SCHOOL-HOME CONNECTION
Help your child write a note using
several abbreviations.

75

Extra Support
Just for You

Name _____

▶ **Write the letters *ar* to complete each picture name.**

1. st _____

2. f _____ m

3. c _____

4. j _____

5. p _____ k

6. _____ m

7. b _____ k

8. ch _____ m

9. al _____ m

SCHOOL-HOME CONNECTION On a sheet of
paper, list the headings –ar, –arm, –ark. Look
through books and magazines for words containing
these letter combinations. Ask your child to write
them on the list under the correct heading.

Extra Support
Just for You

Name _____

▶ **The picture names in each row rhyme. Write the rhyming words. Then write another rhyming word. Draw a picture for it.**

far		
1. _____	_____	_____

harm		
2. _____	_____	_____

spark		
3. _____	_____	_____

SCHOOL-HOME CONNECTION Build rhyming sentences with your child, using words from this lesson. Think of sentences such as, "I took a walk to the (blank) when I heard a dog begin to (blank)." Ask your child to fill in the blanks with rhyming words.

78

Extra Support
Just for You

Name _____

▶ **Circle the correct answer. Then write the answer on the line.**

announced	arrived	glum	members	rebuild

1. You **rebuild** the gate. Do you
take it down or **build it again** ?

_____

2. You are **glum** because it is raining. Are you
sad or **happy**?

_____

3. Your friends are **members** of the Tree House Club.
Are they **part of the club** or **not part of the club**?

_____

4. You **arrived** late. Did you **come late** or **leave late**?

_____

5. The teacher **announced** the winner. Did the teacher
tell **everyone** or **no one**?

_____

 TRY THIS! Write sentences that tell what you would sell at your own stand. Use Vocabulary Words in your writing.

Name _____

▶ **Find the word that has the same sound as the underlined letters in the first word.**

Example: f<u>ar</u>

○ fare

○ care

○ mark

1 ch<u>ar</u>m

○ farm

○ share

○ fall

💡 **Tip**
Read all of the choices before you choose one.

2 p<u>ar</u>k

○ tank

○ bake

○ sparkle

💡 **Tip**
Use what you know about spelling patterns. Compare the sounds.

3 st<u>ar</u>light

○ darkness

○ stare

○ hear

💡 **Tip**
Break a long word into syllables and sound it out.

Name _____

Read the paragraph. Then complete the chart.

Jen and Marco wanted to see the fish at the museum. Both
worked to pay for a ticket. Jen sold drinks. Marco delivered
newspapers. Jen worked alone. Marco worked with his brother.
By Friday, both had earned $15. On Saturday, they went to the
museum together!

Jen	Marco	Both
sold drinks. worked alone.	delivered newspapers. worked with his brother.	wanted to go to the museum. **1.** _____ to pay for a ticket. **2.** _____ $15. **3.** _____ _____

SCHOOL-HOME CONNECTION Talk with your
child about two family friends. Help your child
write about one way the friends are alike and one
way they are different.

Extra Support
Just for You

Name _____

▶ **Look at the chart and the graph. Then answer the questions.**

Number of cups of apple juice sold each week

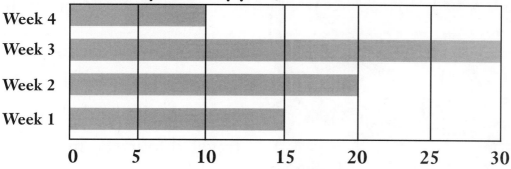

Week 4						
Week 3						
Week 2						
Week 1						

0   5   10   15   20   25   30

1 How many cups were sold in Week 1?

○ 20 cups

○ 10 cups

○ 15 cups

2 In which week were 20 cups sold?

○ Week 1

○ Week 2

○ Week 3

3 When was the most apple juice sold?

○ Week 4

○ Week 3

○ Week 2

💡 Tip

The numbers on the bottom of the chart show the number of cups sold. Each week is shown on the side of the chart. Read each answer choice. First find the week. Then read across to find the number of cups sold in that week.

💡 Tip

Remember that the length of the bar tells how many cups of apple juice were sold. Start with Week 1 at the top of the chart. Look at the number on the bottom of the chart to help you find how many cups were sold.

SCHOOL-HOME CONNECTION Help your child keep track of how many hours he or she sleeps each night for four nights. Then work together to make a bar graph like the one on this page to show this information.

Extra Support
Just for You

Name _____

▶ **Read the story. Circle all the words with *our*. Write all of the words on the chart.**

Four Mice

Four mice went to court. It was the source of all the cheese in the land. They traveled fourteen miles to get there. Of course, they were tired when they arrived. They poured themselves cups of hot tea and went to bed.

1.	
2.	
3.	
4.	
5.	
6.	

SCHOOL-HOME CONNECTION Work with your child to create a four-line poem, using words from this lesson.

84

Extra Support
Just for You

Name _____

▶ **Circle and write the word that completes the sentence.**

1.  You see with your eyes and

_____ with your ears.

hair
hear
head

2. December is the last month

of the _____ .

year
you
your

3.  That man looks strange with

those birds in his _____ .

bean
beard
bell

4.  I really like to _____
my bike.

steer
stair
steam

5.  The _____ from
the crowd were very loud.

chairs
chalk
cheers

6.  I wonder why there are no

people _____ .

nighttime
nearby
new

SCHOOL-HOME CONNECTION Work with your
child to make up rhymes using some of the words
from this lesson. Don't be afraid to make them silly!

85

Extra Support
Just for You

Name _____

▶ **Write the word that makes each sentence tell about the picture.**

| nearby | steer | clearing | reindeer | pioneer | years |

1. Johnny Appleseed was a

_____ .

2. He slept in a

_____ on the grass.

3. He liked to have his animal

friends _____ .

4. The moose and the

_____ were his friends.

5. He lived off the land for

many _____ .

6. He would _____

clear of towns and camp outdoors.

🚒 **SCHOOL-HOME CONNECTION** With your child, use words from this lesson to create a short story about a famous pioneer.

87

Extra Support
Just for You

▶ **Write a Vocabulary Word from the box to complete each unfinished sentence.**

frontier	nearby	orchards	survive	tame	wild

1. You will not find a city or a lot of people here.

You are on the _____.

2. Apple trees grow in these places.

They grow in _____.

3. Bev stands close to Justin.

Bev stands _____.

4. Those rabbits live in the woods.

They are _____.

5. This rabbit is a pet in the classroom. It was easy to

_____.

6. The strong deer live through the cold winter. They

_____.

TRY THIS! Pretend that you are camping with your family. Make a postcard. Write to a friend about your trip. Use as many Vocabulary Words as you can.

Extra Support
Just for You

Johnny Appleseed

R-controlled vowels:
/ir/ ear, eer
TEST PREP

▶ **Mark the word that has the same sound as the underlined letters in the first word.**

Example: d<u>ee</u>r

- ○ dare
- ● clear
- ○ hair

1 ch<u>ee</u>r

- ○ hear
- ○ chair
- ○ care

💡 **Tip**
Listen only to the sound of the letters underlined.

2 y<u>ea</u>rly

- ○ yawn
- ○ deer
- ○ heard

💡 **Tip**
Read the whole word. Listen closely to the part with the underlined letters.

3 engin<u>ee</u>r

- ○ fearless
- ○ parent
- ○ scare

SCHOOL-HOME CONNECTION Say pairs of words for your child that contain similar sounds, for example, *here* and *bear*. Have him or her tell which word contains /ir/.

90

Extra Support
Just for You

Name _____

▶ **Read the story. Then choose the best answer to each question. Fill in the circle next to your choice.**

Johnny's Hat

Johnny Appleseed sometimes wore a pot on his head. The pot was gray with a long handle. The handle was curved. Johnny wore the pot to keep his head dry. It fit his head just right.

1 Johnny's pot was
- ○ blue.
- ○ white.
- ○ black.
- ○ gray.

 Tip
Look for the words *The pot was* in the paragraph. Reread the sentence that describes the color of the pot.

2 How did the pot fit Johnny's head?
- ○ The pot fit just right.
- ○ The pot was too small.
- ○ The pot was too big.
- ○ The pot was too heavy.

Tip
Look for the word *fit* in the paragraph. The answer is nearby.

SCHOOL-HOME CONNECTION With your child, talk about the clothing he or she will wear to school tomorrow. Help your child write sentences using details to describe the clothing.

91

Extra Support
Just for You

Name _____

▶ **Write words from the box to complete the poem. Remember that the word you write should rhyme with the last word in the sentence above.**

far	star	dark	charm

I opened a covered jar.

Inside I found a big white

_____.

It was so bright, it lit up our farm.

It sparkled like a lucky

_____.

I took my star inside the car.

I took my star close and

_____.

I took my star to the park

Wherever I went, it was never

_____.

SCHOOL-HOME CONNECTION With your child, write a diary entry from the point of view of a pioneer. Use all of the *ar*, *arm*, and *ark* words in the box above.

92

Extra Support
Just for You

Name _____

▶ **Choose the word with *spr, str,* or *thr* that names the picture. Write the word on the line.**

1.  string sing strong	**2.**  string sing strong	**3.**  straw strip strap
_____	_____	_____
4.  tree three spree	**5.**  throw three throat	**6.** thread throne tread
_____	_____	_____
7. sprout pout spout	**8.** stitch ostrich stretch	**9.** stay stray spray
_____	_____	_____
10. stream steam team	**11.**  throne throw through	**12.**  spring stroller streams
_____	_____	_____

SCHOOL-HOME CONNECTION Write the letters
spr, str, and *thr* with marker or crayon on a large
sheet of paper. Look through books, magazines, or
newspapers for words beginning with these letters.
Ask your child to write the words under the
appropriate headings.

93

Name _____

▶ **Read the word. Circle the picture whose name has the same consonant sound as the underlined letters.**

1. <u>th</u>rough

2. <u>sp</u>ring

3. <u>str</u>ong

▶ **Write the word that completes each sentence.**

4. The _____ grew to be a big tree.

    sprout   **spray**   **strap**

5. The fish were swimming in the _____.

    straw   **steam**   **stream**

6. I have a sore _____.

    throne   **throat**   **three**

SCHOOL-HOME CONNECTION Write the following word parts on a sheet of paper: __ap; __ay; __ee; __out. Ask your child to add *spr, str,* or *thr* to form words from this lesson. Then invite your child to write sentences using the words.

95

Extra Support
Just for You

▶ **Write a Vocabulary Word from the box to complete each unfinished sentence.**

| beautiful | nutrition | protects | ripens | streams |

1. These flowers have pretty colors. These flowers are

_____ .

2. A banana tastes sweet. A banana tastes best after it

_____ .

3. Oranges are good for you. Oranges are part of

good _____ .

4. Fruit trees grow near water. Fruit trees grow near

_____ and rivers.

5. A fence keeps your garden safe from animals.

A fence _____ your garden.

TRY THIS! Write three sentences about a plant you would like to grow. Use some of the Vocabulary Words in your sentences.

Extra Support
Just for You

Name _____

Syllable Rule • **When a single consonant is between two vowels, divide before the consonant. Try the first syllable long. If the word makes sense, keep it!**

Example: ti/ger   pa/per

• **If the word doesn't make sense, divide after the consonant and try it short.**

Example: drag/on   vis/it

▶ Read the words. Circle the words that have short vowel sounds. Write the words you circled where they belong.

river

1. _____

travel

2. _____

polar

3. _____

palace

4. _____

broken

5. _____

hotel

6. _____

wagon

7. _____

freezer

8. _____

token

9. _____

ever

10. _____

Extra Support
Just for You

Name _____

▶ **Read the paragraph and the diagram. Then choose the best answer to each question. Fill in the circle next to your choice.**

Germination

A new plant grows from a seed. The sun warms the seed in the ground. Then the seed coat breaks. Roots begin to grow down into the soil. The seed begins to sprout.

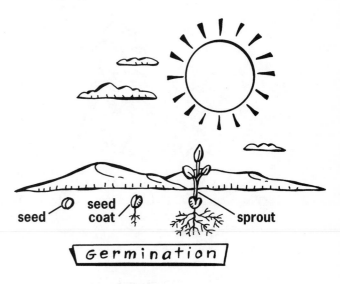

seed   seed coat   sprout

Germination

1 What does the diagram tell you?

○ the name of the new plant

○ the kind of soil

○ how a seed grows

○ the names of insects on leafy plants

💡 **Tip**
Read all of the labels. Then read all of your choices carefully.

2 Use the diagram to help you. Which sentence would go best at the end of the paragraph?

○ Seeds look like small grains or nuts.

○ A shoot and leaves grow toward the sun.

○ Insects feed on plants.

○ Plants have many leaves.

💡 **Tip**
Try reading the paragraph with each answer choice. Then choose the best answer.

Extra Support
Just for You

Name _____

HOMEWORK
From Seed
to Plant

R-controlled
Vowels:
/ir/, ear, eer

► **Read the sentence. Circle the words that contain *ear* or *eer* and sound like *deer* or *hear*. Write the words in the chart.**

The old man with a beard planted flowers every year. He planted the seeds in a clearing nearby. Some people said he was a pioneer. Others gave him cheers. It didn't matter to him because he couldn't hear.

1.	
2.	
3.	
4.	
5.	
6.	
7.	

SCHOOL-HOME CONNECTION With your child, look in newspapers or magazines for words that contain *ear* or *eer*. Invite your child to circle the *ear* and *eer* words.

100

Extra Support
Just for You

Name _____

▶ **Choose the word that names the picture. Write the word on the line.**

1. sooner scooter soup _____	**2.** root rule roof _____	**3.** fun food full _____
4. boot boom boat _____	**5.** baboon balloon boom _____	**6.** hoot hook hoop _____
7. soon spoon soap _____	**8.** roots rules rooms _____	**9.** brook brush broom _____
10. mow move moon _____	**11.** room root rule _____	**12.** tunes tools tones _____

SCHOOL-HOME CONNECTION Ask your child to look through some of his or her books for words containing *oo* with the sound heard in *school*.

101

Extra Support
Just for You

▶ **Write the word from the box that completes
each sentence.**

| roots | food | cartoon | scooter | smooth | boots |

1.		Sam watched a _____.
2.		Then he put on his _____.
3.		He hopped on his _____.
4.		He took the _____ path.
5.		He stopped by a tree with big _____.
6.		Sam had some _____ by the tree.

SCHOOL-HOME CONNECTION Ask your child
to choose five words from this lesson and either
write or tell a story using those five words.

103

Extra Support
Just for You

Name _____

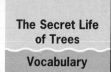

▶ **Read the clues. Match the Vocabulary Words from the box to the clues. Write the correct word on each line.**

discover	energy	forecast	shed	source

1. You listen to this to know what the weather will be tomorrow.

_____

2. You do this when you find something for the first time.

_____

3. You need this to run and jump.

_____

4. This is the place where something begins.

_____

5. Snakes do this with their skin.

_____

TRY THIS! Draw pictures of rainy weather, sunny weather, and snowy weather. Then write a sentence about each of your pictures. Use some of the Vocabulary Words.

Extra Support
Just for You

Syllable Rule • **When a word ends in a consonant and *le*, divide the word before the consonant.**

Example: cir/cle

▶ Read the words in the box. Write each word in syllables where it belongs in the chart. Cross out each word in the box after you write it.

able	babble	candle	idle
rattle	title	fable	uncle

ta/ble   **rip/ple**

1. _____   5. _____

2. _____   6. _____

3. _____   7. _____

4. _____   8. _____

Extra Support
Just for You

Name _____

▶ **Read the book titles and their descriptions.
Then fill in the circle that best answers each
question.**

This book describes
how leaves change
color in the fall.

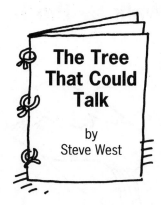

This book tells of a tree
that can talk when fed
purple water.

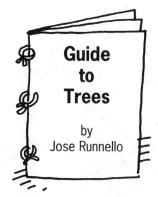

This book gives information
on how to identify trees by
their leaves.

1 Which book is fiction? ————

○ Trees and Their Leaves

○ The Tree That Could Talk

○ Guide to Trees

○ None of the above

💡 **Tip**

For fiction, look for the
book that describes
something that could
not happen in real life.

2 Which book is fact? ————

○ Trees and Their Leaves

○ The Tree That Could Talk

○ Guide to Trees

○ Both Trees and Their Leaves
and Guide to Trees

💡 **Tip**

Read all answers before
making a choice. When
an answer has the word
both, make sure that
both items fit the
question.

SCHOOL-HOME CONNECTION Read excerpts
from a newspaper article and a fairy tale to your
child. Have him or her tell you which is fiction.
Then have your child explain why.

107

Extra Support
Just for You

Name _____

▶ **Read the sentences. Do what they tell you.**
Circle the words that contain *spr*, *str*, or *thr*.

A Walk by the Stream

1. It is springtime. The leaves sprout. Color the leaves green.

2. The waterfall sprays water. Color the water blue.

3. The sun is peeking through the clouds. Color the sun yellow.

4. The streams look cool. Color the fish in the stream.

5. Three ostriches play in the grass. Color the three ostriches.

SCHOOL-HOME CONNECTION After your child completes this page, work together to make up new sentences using words from this lesson.

108

Extra Support
Just for You

Watermelon Day
Consonant
Digraphs: /n/gn,
kn; /r/wr

▶ **Choose the word that names the picture. Write the word on the line.**

1.
knew
knock
knot
_____

2.
gnu
net
gnat
_____

3.
writer
wire
wrong
_____

4.
wren
when
wrinkled
_____

5.
west
wrist
wrong
_____

6.
know
knot
knight
_____

7.
wren
wrong
write
_____

8.
kite
knight
knife
_____

9.
knit
knot
knock
_____

10.
KEEP OFF
GRASS
sign
say
sing
_____

11.
know
knee
knock
_____

SCHOOL-HOME CONNECTION Ask your child
to underline and pronounce the *kn, gn,* or *wr* in
each of the words in this lesson.

109

Extra Support
Just for You

Name _____

Watermelon Day
Consonant
Digraphs: /n/gn,
kn; /r/wr

▶ **Read the word. Circle the picture whose name
has the same two beginning letters as the word.**

1. knew

2. gnu

3. write

▶ **Read the sentences. Write the word that best
completes each one.**

4. I painted the _____ at the park.

        sign   sing   song

5. The location of the secret club is _____.

              ugly   unknown   knight

6. I hurt my _____ playing tennis.

     write   wrong   wrist

SCHOOL-HOME CONNECTION Discuss with your
child different ideas that may help in remembering
how to spell the words from this unit.

111

Extra Support
Just for You

Name _____

▶ **Write a Vocabulary Word from the box to complete each sentence.**

| beneath | relay race | shimmered | snug | wrinkled | knelt |

1. Lisa _____ on her knees to pick berries.

2. Some of the melon was hidden _____ the leaves.

3. The sun made the leaves dry and _____.

4. The lake _____ and sparkled.

5. Our team won the _____.

6. I was _____ and cozy inside my sleeping bag.

 TRY THIS! Write three sentences about a summer activity you enjoy. Use Vocabulary Words. Draw a picture about your sentences.

Name _____

Syllable Rule • **When a word ends in consonant *-le*, divide the word before the consonant.**

ban/gle

• **When a two-syllable word with consonant *-le* adds *-ed*, it changes spelling. The ending becomes part of the second syllable.**

▶ Read the two-syllable words in the box. Then write words in syllables.

| wrinkled | tangled | giggled | sparkled | circled |

C-*le* Words   C-*le* Words with ed

1. sparkle _____

2. giggle _____

3. _____ tangled

4. circle _____

5. wrinkle _____

Name _____

▶ **Read the paragraph. Then choose the best answer to each question. Fill in the circle next to your choice.**

Sammy walked around the corner. He saw ten watermelons all in a row. He also saw peaches near them. A man with an apron was stacking the peaches. Then Sammy heard his father call his name. He ran to join his father at the check-out counter.

1 This story most likely takes place ———
- ○ at Sammy's house.
- ○ at school.
- ○ at the beach.
- ○ at a store.

💡 **Tip**
Where can you see so much fruit? Find the answer that matches your idea.

2 It is most likely that Sammy is ———
- ○ walking home from school.
- ○ buying food with his father.
- ○ walking on the beach.
- ○ on vacation.

💡 **Tip**
What do people do at a check-out counter? Find the answer that matches your idea.

SCHOOL-HOME CONNECTION Read a few sentences from a travel brochure or guide with your child. Help your child look for clue words to make inferences about the place being described.

Extra Support
Just for You

▶ **Read the story. Circle all the words with *ear*. Write all of the words on the chart.**

Early one day when the earth was just waking up, a bird heard a noise. He searched all day to learn where the noise was coming from. Then the bird saw an oyster sitting on a rock, far

from the sea. The bird helped the oyster find his way back to the sea. The oyster was so happy that he gave the bird his shiny pearl. "Here," he said, "you earned it."

1.	
2.	
3.	
4.	
5.	
6.	
7.	

SCHOOL-HOME CONNECTION Using the words *learn, search,* and *earn,* have your child choose one as the word of the day. Ask him or her to learn something, search for something, or try to earn something on a particular day.

116

Extra Support
Just for You

Name _____

▶ **Circle and write the word that completes each sentence.**

1. He _____ while eating French fries.
cry   cries   cities

2. A bird flies in wide open _____.
skies   ski   see

3. She made two _____ of bright red poppies.
color   copy   copies

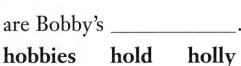

4. Airplanes and stamps

are Bobby's _____.
hobbies   hold   holly

5. These little cuties will

grow up to be _____.
bear   beauty   beauties

6. Clean up your _____
so they don't get gritty.
circus   cities   circle

SCHOOL-HOME CONNECTION Make several
letter y's with a marker or a crayon on small strips
of paper. Then write the phonics words on a
separate page. Ask your child to cover the *-ies* with
the y and point out how it changes the meaning of the word.
(The word becomes singular.)

117

Extra Support
Just for You

▶ **Write the word that makes each sentence tell about the picture.**

| hobbies | studies | cries | pennies | babies | duties |

1. Bill and Lourdes have _____.

2. Sue collects _____.

3. Sue has many _____, too.

4. She _____ her spelling words.

5. She takes care of _____.

6. Sue holds the baby when

he _____.

SCHOOL-HOME CONNECTION Ask your child to circle each word on this page with the *-ies* ending.

119

Extra Support
Just for You

Name _____

▶ **Draw a line from each Vocabulary Word on the left to its meaning on the right.**

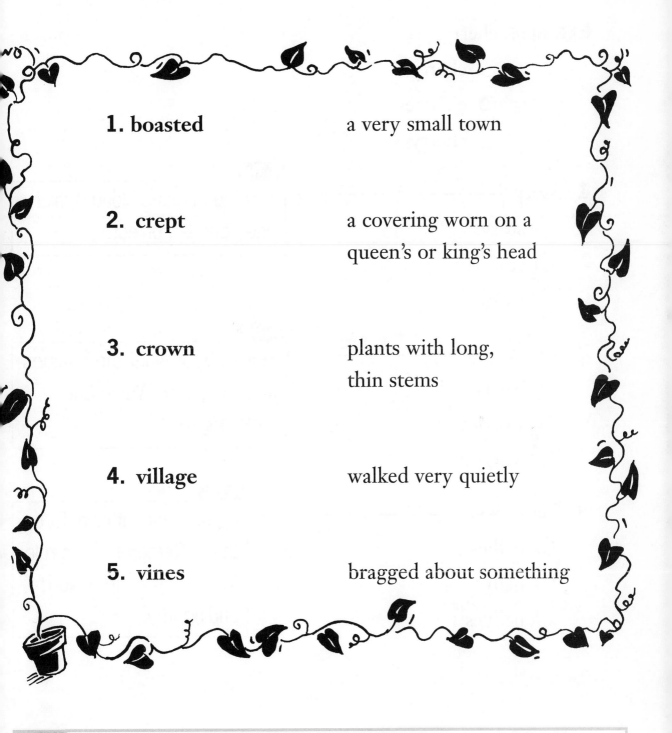

1. boasted   a very small town

2. crept   a covering worn on a
                                    queen's or king's head

3. crown   plants with long,
                                    thin stems

4. village   walked very quietly

5. vines   bragged about something

TRY THIS! Write three sentences about your favorite holiday. Use as many Vocabulary Words as possible.

120

Extra Support
Just for You

▶ **Find the word that is spelled correctly. Fill in the circle next to the answer you chose.**

Example cherry

     ○ cherrys

     ● cherries

     ○ cherryes

1 story

     ○ storys

     ○ storyes

     ○ stories

💡 **Tip**

Say the choices aloud. Which one sounds correct?

2 worry

     ○ worrys

     ○ worries

     ○ worryes

💡 **Tip**

Think about what the choices look like, too. Which one looks right?

3 belly

     ○ bellies

     ○ bellys

     ○ bellyes

💡 **Tip**

Look at the letter before the *y*. Remember the rule for adding –*s* to a word ending in *y*.

Name _____

▶ **Here is how Mack began a letter. Read it and think about what happens next. Then answer each question.**

Dear Grandma,

   Do you remember the carrot seeds you sent us? Mom and I planted them in our garden. Then we watered them a lot. You told me to talk to them. I said, "Grow, carrots. Grow!" I checked those carrot seeds every day for weeks. Nothing happened. I wanted to tell you, "Those seeds are no good." Then, this morning something happened. You won't believe what I found.

1. What do you think Mack found?

💡 **Tip**
Think of what you know about planting seeds.

_____

_____

2. What story clues helped you predict what happened?

💡 **Tip**
Think about what is being described. Read again about what Mack does to the seeds.

_____

_____

_____

3. Do you think Mack will tell his mother?

💡 **Tip**
Think about Mack's feelings. Is he excited?

_____

SCHOOL-HOME CONNECTION Work with your child to make up the first part of a story about an unusual plant. Talk about what might happen at the end. Then ask your child to tell you an ending for the story.

Extra Support
Just for You

▶ **Read the sentences. Circle the words that contain *our*.**

1. The waterfall is the source
of the river.

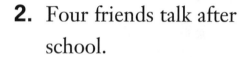

2. Four friends talk after
school.

3. The rain poured, but
Connor stayed dry.

4. Fourteen butterflies
fly in the sky.

5. Each butterfly stays
on course.

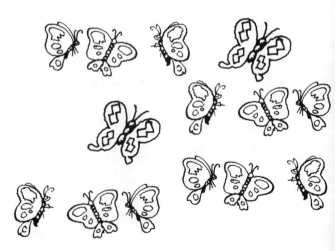

 SCHOOL-HOME CONNECTION Ask your child
"What is your favorite thing to do when it pours?"
Talk with your child about fun things to do on a
rainy day.

124

Extra Support
Just for You

• TROPHIES •

Volume Two

Banner Days

▶ **Write the letters *ou* or *ow* to complete each picture name.**

1. m _____ th   **2.** br _____   **3.** _____ t

4. cl _____ n   **5.** s _____ nd   **6.** c _____

7. cr _____ n   **8.** ar _____ nd   **9.** g _____ n

10. h _____ se **11.** fr _____ n **12.** f _____ nd

SCHOOL-HOME CONNECTION Work with your child to keep a running list of *ow* and *ou* words. Add to the list as you discover new words.

1

Extra Support
Banner Days

Name _____

▶ **Write the word that makes each sentence tell about the picture.**

| how | without | now | found | house | around |

1. Bobby lost his boa in the _____.

2. _____ will he find it?

3. He looks _____ the chair.

4. _____ what should he do?

5. The boa would not go _____ his stuffed bear.

6. Bobby has _____ him!

SCHOOL-HOME CONNECTION Ask your child
to circle all the words on this page containing /ou/
spelled *ou* or *ow*.

3

Extra Support
Banner Days

Name _____

▶ **Write a Vocabulary Word from the box to
complete each sentence.**

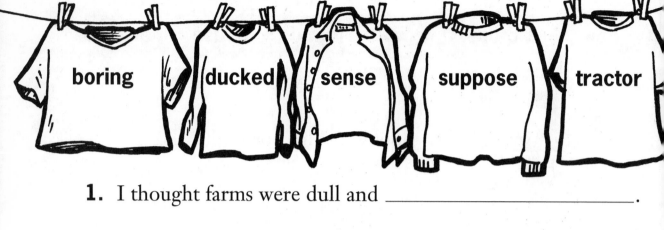

boring   ducked   sense   suppose   tractor

1. I thought farms were dull and _____.

2. I _____ under the clothesline.

3. We saw a _____ carrying a heavy load.

4. I _____ it was soil. What's your guess?

5. That makes _____. I think you are
right.

**TRY
THIS!**

Pretend your class is on a field trip at a farm. Write a story
about what you do. Use as many Vocabulary Words as you
can in your sentences.

| Syllable Rule | • **If a word has an ending such as** |

ly, divide the word between the base word and the ending.

Examples: glad/ly   help/less   fast/er

▶ **On the line, write the bold word in syllables to complete the sentence.**

1. Rocky barks _____
   loudly
   when the doorbell rings.

2. He likes _____ long walks
   taking
   with me.

3. He is a _____ dog.
   fearless

4. Rocky is _____ when he plays.
   careful

5. He is the _____ dog in the
   nicest
   whole world!

Name _____

▶ **Read the story. Then complete the sentences.**

The Rainy Day .

It was a rainy day at school. We could not play outside. The playground was soaked. After lunch, we walked back to the classroom. There we saw markers, paints, and crayons on our desks. Our teacher smiled. It was time for arts and crafts. Everyone was excited.

1 The children could not play outside because

_____

_____ .

> **Tip**
> A cause is why something happened. Often the cause happens right before the effect.

2 Everyone was excited because

_____

_____ .

> **Tip**
> An effect is what happened because of something else.

SCHOOL-HOME CONNECTION With your child, read a newspaper article. Help your child figure out a cause and an effect of the event described.

7

Extra Support
Banner Days

Name _____

▶ **Write the word that makes each sentence tell about the picture.**

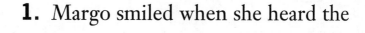

harmful	hairless	lifeless	starless
mouthful	joyful	restful	cloudless

1. Margo smiled when she heard the

_____ news.

2. The baby's head looks _____ .

3. We spent a _____ day at the beach.

4. Len took a _____ of food.

5. Be careful. That snake looks

_____ .

6. It was a _____ night.

7. The sky was _____ , and the sun was bright.

8. The tree seemed old and _____ .

SCHOOL-HOME CONNECTION With your child, make up sentences with words that end with –ful or –less, such as *truthful, careful, nameless,* and *timeless.* Talk about the base words: *truth, care, name,* and *time.* Ask your child how the ending –ful or –less changes the meaning of the root word.

8

Extra Support
Banner Days

▶ **Read the story. Circle all the words with *oo*. Write all of the words on the chart.**

I like to ride my scooter to school. I have fun there. We learn about trees with smooth leaves and big roots. We also learn about the moon. Then we eat yummy food, like watermelon. I use a spoon to eat. Later, I help clean the room with a broom.

1.
2.
3.
4.
5.
6.
7.
8.
9.

SCHOOL-HOME CONNECTION Review the words from this lesson with your child. Practice spelling these words together.

9

Extra Support
Banner Days

Name _____

▶ **Circle and write the word that completes each sentence.**

1. The hats are too small for

the _____.

cows
cowboys
coins

2. Katy gets much

_____ from dancing.

jay
join
joy

3. I have only one more

_____ left.

coin
cane
cone

4. You must put _____
in a car to keep it running.

all
ill
oil

5. We use our _____
to sing.

vases
verse
voices

6. Tasha will _____ to
number one.

point
paint
pint

SCHOOL-HOME CONNECTION Have your
child point out the words with the *oi* sound. Work
together to make up new sentences with these
words. Have your child draw a picture to illustrate
the new sentences.

10

Extra Support
Banner Days

Name _____

▶ **Read each word. Circle the picture that has a name with the same vowel sound.**

1. joy

2. join

3. boil

▶ **Read the sentences. Write the word that best completes each one.**

4. Did you plant the seeds in the _____?

                sail   soil   seal

5. I put the popcorn in the hot _____.

                oil   all   ill

6. I get much _____ from riding horses.

     engine   enjoyment   edge

SCHOOL-HOME CONNECTION Discuss the *oi*
sound in the word *noise* with your child. Have your
child listen as you call out words from this page.
If you say a word with the *oi* sound, tell your child
to make a funny noise.

12

► **Write a Vocabulary Word from the box to complete each sentence.**

captured	imagination	manners	matador
plains	relax	vacation	

1. If you caught something, you _____ it.

2. When you say "please" and
   "thank you," you use good

   _____ .

3. You use your _____
   to think about something you have never seen.

4. _____ are large, flat
   areas of land.

5. The time when we don't go to
   school in the summer is called a

   _____ .

6. A _____ fights bulls.

7. When you _____, you feel calm.

TRY THIS! What kind of vacation would you like to go on? Write
sentences about your dream vacation. Use as many
Vocabulary Words as you can.

▶ **Choose the word with the same sound as the underlined letters in the first word.**

Example j<u>oi</u>n

● toy

○ boat

○ top

1 c<u>oi</u>n

○ crown

○ room

○ boy

> **Tip**
> Say the word and listen to the sound that the underlined letters make.

2 enj<u>oy</u>

○ corner

○ book

○ point

> **Tip**
> Remember that *oi* and *oy* make the same sound.

3 b<u>oi</u>led

destroy

○ butter

○ bother

> **Tip**
> Ignore any word choices that don't make sense.

Name _____

▶ **Read the story. Then fill in the chart of causes and effects.**

I had the day off from school. I was going to play soccer, but it rained. I stayed at home instead. I decided to give my dog a bath. We didn't have any dog shampoo, so I washed her with toothpaste. She seemed pretty clean, but her fur was kind of sticky. I had to give her another bath with human shampoo. Now her fur is shiny.

Cause	Effect
_____	The narrator stayed at home.
_____	
There was no dog shampoo.	_____
	_____
The dog's fur was sticky.	_____
	_____

SCHOOL-HOME CONNECTION Play a cause-and-effect game with your child. Ask your child what he or she would have done today if it had snowed, been sunny, or rained ice cream. Make up as many funny effects as you can.

16

Extra Support
Banner Days

Name _____

How I Spent My
Summer Vacation

Review:
R-controlled
vowels: /ir/
ear, eer

▶ **Read the story. Circle all the words with *ear* or *eer*. Write all of the words on the chart. Write each word only once.**

Reindeer liked his home in the woods. He lived in a clearing.

Deer lived nearby. Each year when the days turned cold Deer and

Reindeer grew long beards. When they walked into town, they

could hear the cheers of their friends.

1.	
2.	
3.	
4.	
5.	
6.	
7.	
8.	

SCHOOL-HOME CONNECTION Ask your child to think of a cheer using two or three words from this exercise.

17

Extra Support
Banner Days

Name _____

▶ **Choose the word that names the picture.**
Write the word on the line.

1.
goal
glue
girl

_____

2.
mine
main
moon

_____

3.
boil
blue
bowl

_____

4.
name
nine
noon

_____

5.
reef
roof
raft

_____

6.
pole
pail
pool

_____

7.
round
room
roam

_____

8.
zipper
zing
zoo

_____

9.
spoon
soap
spine

_____

10.
tool
toil
tail

_____

11.
boat
bait
boot

_____

12.
mice
mouse
moose

_____

SCHOOL-HOME CONNECTION Have your
child choose four of the pictures on this page.
With your child, write a few sentences about the
pictures using words with *oo* or *ue*. Have your
child underline the words that have the *oo* sound.

Extra Support
Banner Days

▶ **Write the word that makes each sentence tell about the picture.**

too	clue	noon	due	soon	true

1. Jen is _____ to come at twelve o'clock.

2. She is bringing her pet goldfish at

_____.

3. Is it _____ that goldfish eat special food?

4. Seth has a pet goldfish _____.

5. Seth hopes Jen will give him a

_____.

6. Jen will be at Seth's house _____.

SCHOOL-HOME CONNECTION Discuss the hours on a clock with your child. Have your child show you where the clock hands would be when it is noon. Ask your child to think of words that rhyme with noon.

20

Extra Support
Banner Days

► **Draw a line from each Vocabulary Word on the left to its correct meaning on the right.**

1. details   to let down

2. disappoint   to pet or rub

3. forcibly   small pieces
                               of information

4. information   large bodies of salt water

5. oceans   very strongly

6. stroke   facts or knowledge

 TRY THIS! Many different creatures live in the ocean. Choose one, and write two or three sentences about it. Use as many Vocabulary Words as you can.

Name _____

| **Syllable Rule** | • **Divide a compound word** |

between the two smaller words in it.
Examples: hot/dog   sail/boat

▶ Read the words in the box. Write each word in syllables.

blackboard	baseball	bookstore
whenever	backpack	healthcare
anything	headband	football

Compound Words

1. _____   4. _____   7. _____

2. _____   5. _____   8. _____

3. _____   6. _____   9. _____

▶ Write a sentence for three of the words.

10. _____

_____

11. _____

_____

12. _____

_____

Name _____

▶ **Read the paragraph. Then choose the best answer to each question. Fill in the circle next to your choice.**

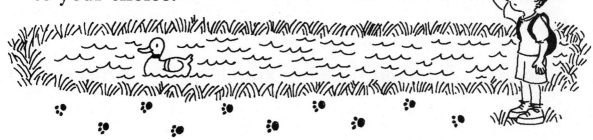

Leisha walked to the pond to look for her dog, Tricks. There were wet dog tracks leading from the pond to the grass. Leisha followed the tracks. Then she heard a bark. It was Tricks! He was soaking wet. She quickly pulled a towel out of her backpack.

1 Most likely, Tricks was wet because

- ○ he played in the sprinklers.
- ○ it rained.
- ○ he ran under a water hose.
- ○ he swam in the pond.

2 Which part of the paragraph helped you with the first question?

- ○ Leisha walked to the pond.
- ○ There were wet dog tracks leading from the pond.
- ○ Leisha followed the tracks.
- ○ She quickly pulled a towel out of her backpack.

💡 **Tip**

Reread the paragraph. Find out where the water is in the story.

💡 **Tip**

Look for the answer that makes the most sense.

SCHOOL-HOME CONNECTION Read a favorite story with your child. Help your child use story clues to make inferences about the characters and setting.

24

Extra Support
Banner Days

▶ **Write the word from the box that best completes the poem. Remember that the word you write should rhyme with the sentence or phrase above it.**

gnat	knife	knock	write

A little gnu was sitting on a rock.

First she heard a voice, and then she heard a

_____ .

She was surprised and said, "Look at that!"

Knocking on her rock was a wee little _____ .

The little gnat was quite a sight,

Especially when he started to _____ .

He asked for some pie for his little gnat wife,

So the gnu cut a slice with her plastic _____ .

SCHOOL-HOME CONNECTION Ask your child to find rhyming words for the following three words from this lesson: *write, knock,* and *gnat.*

25

Extra Support
Banner Days

Name _____

▶ **Choose the word that names the picture.**
Write the word on the line.

1.

shelf
shelves
shoves

_____

2.

lives
leaf
leaves

_____

3.

shovel
shelves
shelfs

_____

4.

calf
cuff
calves

_____

5.

halfs
halves
heavy

_____

6.

elfs
elevate
elves

_____

7.

wifes
wolf
wives

_____

8.

leafs
loaves
leaves

_____

9.

waffle
wife
wive

_____

10.

eel
elves
elf

_____

11.

have
half
halves

_____

12.

calfs
caves
calves

_____

SCHOOL-HOME CONNECTION Cut an apple or
other piece of fruit in half and share it with your child.
Discuss the words *half* and *halves*. Have your child
write the words and explain the spelling change.

26

Extra Support
Banner Days

Name _____

▶ **Read each sentence. Write the word that completes each sentence.**

| life | half | halves | leaf | lives | leaves |

1. Marta likes to draw pictures about

her _____.

2. She draws pictures of _____ falling from trees.

3. One _____ lands on her notebook.

4. Mom gives her _____ an orange.

5. Dad brings in more orange _____.

6. Maybe Marta will draw a picture about

their _____ too.

SCHOOL-HOME CONNECTION With your child, discuss important events in his or her life. Help your child make a timeline outlining some of these events.

28

Extra Support
Banner Days

▶ **Draw a line from the Vocabulary Word on the right to the word on the left that means almost the same thing.**

1. copied

2. cried

3. white

4. liked

5. see

6. mist

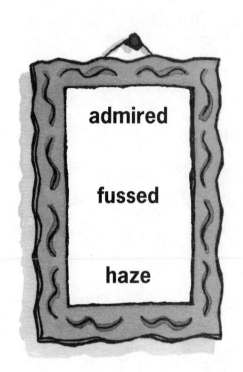

admired

fussed

haze

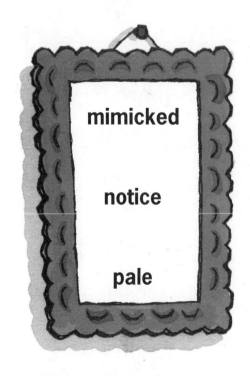

mimicked

notice

pale

 TRY THIS! Write a paragraph about a person you admire. Use as many Vocabulary Words as you can.

Syllable Rule • **Divide a compound word between the two smaller words in it.**

Examples: hot/dog   sail/boat

▶ **Read the words in the box. Write each word in syllables.**

birthday	horseshoe	daydream
broadcast	rainbow	sidewalk
moonlight	sunshine	catfish
pinpoint	footstep	keyhole

Compound Word

1. _____   5. _____   9. _____

2. _____   6. _____   10. _____

3. _____   7. _____   11. _____

4. _____   8. _____   12. _____

Name _____

▶ **Read the paragraph. Then choose the best answer to each question. Fill in the circle next to your choice.**

Judy liked to paint. She painted pictures of her family on paper. She painted a picture of a <u>happy</u> frog with a smile on his face. She painted a <u>light</u> blue star on a dark blue chair.

1 An antonym for *happy* is—
- ○ joyful
- ○ glad
- ○ sad
- ○ merry

💡 **Tip**

Antonyms have opposite meanings. Find the word that means "not happy"?

2 An antonym for *light* is—
- ○ dark
- ○ clear
- ○ white
- ○ bright

💡 **Tip**

Look for the opposite of *light*.

SCHOOL-HOME CONNECTION With your child, make a list of a few words and their antonyms. Discuss the differences between the meanings.

32

Extra Support
Banner Days

Name _____

▶ **Read the story. Circle all the abbreviations.**
Write them on the chart.

Horse and Duck are best friends.

Each Sun. they play in the stream. On

Tues. they run in the grass. On Wed.

they walk to town to see Dr. Brown. In

Jan. Mr. Bibbs gives them nice warm

blankets. In Aug. he brings them new

straw hats.

1. _____

2. _____

3. _____

4. _____

5. _____

6. _____

7. _____

SCHOOL-HOME CONNECTION With your child,
look through a calendar to find abbreviations for the
days of the week and the months of the year. Invite
your child to tell what each abbreviation stands for.

33

Extra Support
Banner Days

▶ **Read each sentence. Circle and write the word that completes each sentence.**

1. The penguin is _____ with its friends.

swim
swimming
swims

2. Lin is _____ breakfast.

eating
eats
eat

3. The baby is _____ covered in mud.

completed
complete
completely

4. Ted is _____ telling jokes on stage.

actual
actually
acting

5. It is _____ to rain on the parade.

started
start
starting

6. Maya _____ walked to school.

slowing
slowly
slowed

SCHOOL-HOME CONNECTION Have your child draw several pictures of penguins engaged in different activities—swimming, eating, standing, etc. Discuss the pictures and have your child write a sentence about each, using words that end in –*ing* and –*ly*.

Extra Support
Banner Days

Name _____

▶ **Read each sentence. Write the word that
completes each sentence.**

| doing | taking | pouring |
| standing | completely | freezing |

1. Matt is _____ his homework.

2. He is _____ water into a tray.

3. The water is _____ into ice.

4. Matt is _____ his ice cubes to school.

5. He is _____ in line to go inside.

6. Matt's homework has _____ melted!

SCHOOL-HOME CONNECTION Make two columns on a piece of paper. Write –ly at the top of one column and –ing at the top of the second column. With your child, list as many words as possible with these two word endings.

36

Extra Support
Banner Days

▶ **Draw a line from the Vocabulary Word on the left to its meaning on the right.**

flippers　　　**1.** causing sliding

hatch　　　**2.** very sad

horizon　　　**3.** to come from an egg

miserable　　　**4.** broad, flat limbs used for swimming

slippery　　　**5.** walked swaying from side to side

waddled　　　**6.** the place where the land meets the sky

 TRY THIS! Write a letter to a friend telling about a day you went on vacation. Use Vocabulary Words.

▶ **Choose the word in which *–ing* or *–ly* is added correctly.**

Example win

     ○ wining   ○ winning   ○ wineing

1 extreme

     ○ extremly

     ○ extremmly

     ○ extremely

> **Tip**
> Say each choice to yourself.

2 run

     ○ running

     ○ runeing

     ○ runing

> **Tip**
> Think about the rules before you choose. What do you know about adding **–ing** to a word?

3 trace

     ○ tracing

     ○ traceing

     ○ traccing

> **Tip**
> What do you know about adding **–ing** to a word that ends with a silent **e**?

Name _____

▶ **Read the book titles and their descriptions.
Then answer the questions. Write your
answers on the lines.**

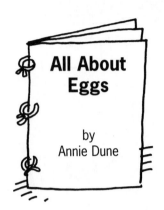

**All About
Eggs**

by
Annie Dune

**Bird
Watching**

by
Emma Gordon

**Bird
Tales**

by
Jeff Greene

This book describes the
eggs of many different
birds. Photos are
included.

This book gives
information about where
to find different kinds of
birds. It includes maps
and diagrams.

This book tells of a
talking penguin and his
adventures on the
Arctic ice.

1 Which books are nonfiction? ———

_____

_____

> **Tip**
> Photos are used
> often for nonfiction

2 Which book is fiction? ———

_____

_____

> **Tip**
> For fiction, look
> for the book that
> describes
> something that
> could not happen
> in real life.

SCHOOL-HOME CONNECTION With your child,
read a favorite story. Ask your child whether the
story is fact or fiction.

40

Extra Support
Banner Days

▶ **Read the story. Circle all the words with *-ies*.
Write all the words on the chart.**

City Chicks

Three little chicks who were just babies

walked into the city one day. "Cities scare

me," said one little chick. "I'm hungry," said

another. "I have some pennies," said a third.

"Maybe we can buy some cookies." "Let's get

those. They are beauties!" The chicks ate.

Then they walked back home to play with

their toys and do other hobbies.

1.	
2.	
3.	
4.	
5.	
6.	

SCHOOL-HOME CONNECTION With your child, write or tell a short story about traveling somewhere. Circle or write down all the plural words you use in your story.

41

Extra Support
Banner Days

► **Circle and write the word that begins with *re–*
or *pre–* and completes each sentence.**

1. The birds _____ the
string from the ground.

remove
removes
moves

2. Does a fish go to

_____?

preschool
school
preplan

3. I will _____ my
small bike with a bigger one.

place
replace
preplace

4. We watched an exciting movie

_____.

preview
view
viewing

5. A _____ comes at
the beginning of a word.

refix
prefix
fix

6. I can't _____ your
phone number.

precall
caller
recall

SCHOOL-HOME CONNECTION Ask your child
to think of two other words that have the prefixes
re- or *pre-*. Have your child use the words in
sentences that tell what each word means.

Extra Support
Banner Days

Name _____

▶ **Write the word that makes each sentence tell about the picture.**

repack	return	recycle	prepay	preheat	retie

1. My aunt will _____ the oven.

2. Did you _____ the toys to the box?

3. Mary needs to _____ her backpack.

4. Brian has to _____ his sneakers.

5. Uncle Bruno will _____ for his gas at the station.

6. We always _____ our cans and bottles.

🚒 **SCHOOL-HOME CONNECTION** Have your child tell you the difference between the words *preheat* and *reheat*. Ask your child to explain when and why you would do each of these things.

44

Extra Support
Banner Days

Name _____

▶ **Complete each sentence. Write a Vocabulary Word from the box on each line.**

caused	clasp	confused	cornered
objects	removes	typical	

1. _____ are also called "things".

2. If you made something happen, you _____ it.

3. If Maria takes something away, she _____ it.

4. If you are mixed up, you are _____.

5. If I am just like all the others, I am _____.

6. A _____ holds objects or parts together.

7. If you chase the cat into the closet, you have _____ it.

TRY THIS! Movies can be funny, scary, sad, or exciting. Write a paragraph about your favorite movie. Use as many Vocabulary Words as you can.

Extra Support
Banner Days

Name _____

Syllable Rule • **When a word has a prefix, divide the word between the prefix and base word. Examples:** *re/read un/kind*

▶ **On the line, write the bold word, dividing it into syllables.**

1. We will ___pre/view___ the show.

   preview

2. I will _____ my old hometown.

   revisit

3. That rule is _____.

   unfair

4. I will _____ the directions.

   reread

5. Maggie will _____ the ribbon.

   untie

Name _____

▶ **Read the story. Then choose the best answer
to each question. Fill in the circle next to
your choice.**

The Mystery of the Missing Baseball Glove

John could not find his baseball glove. His game was in
an hour. He ran all around the house looking for the glove.
He looked under his bed. He looked under
the table. Finally, he looked under
his cat, Smoke. Smoke was
sleeping on the glove!

1. What is the problem in this story's plot?
- ○ John likes to play baseball.
- ○ John has a cat named Smoke.
- ○ John has a baseball game.
- ○ John lost his baseball glove.

> **💡 Tip**
> Most stories tell
> the main problem
> at the beginning.
> Look there first.

2 How is the problem solved?
- ○ John finds the glove under his bed.
- ○ John finds the glove under the table.
- ○ John finds the glove under the cat.
- ○ John finds the glove in his backpack.

> **💡 Tip**
> Look at the end
> of the story. It
> often tells how
> the problem is
> solved.

SCHOOL-HOME CONNECTION With your child,
make up a story about someone who has lost
something. Ask your child to tell you the story's
main problem and how it is solved.

48

▶ **Circle and write the word that completes each sentence.**

1. She _____ her jewelry case.

place
misplaced
misty

2. The _____ was green and lush.

brush
unhappy
underbrush

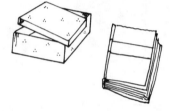

3. The man _____ the box for his book.

mister
mystery
mistook

4. I like to _____ words when I read.

underline
untied
united

5. The turtle was the _____ in the race.

underdog
dogsled
understand

6. The _____ dog wanted to eat.

undone
underfed
underfood

SCHOOL-HOME CONNECTION With your child write a list of words that begin with *mis–* or *under–*. Circle the base word in each example. Ask your child to choose three words and write two sentences for each word. Invite your child to use the base word in one sentence and the word with a prefix in the second sentence. Discuss how the meanings of sentence are alike and different.

49

Name _____

The Pine Park
Mystery

Review:
Vowel Diphthongs:
/ou/ *ou, ow*

► **On the line write the words from the box that
best complete the poem. Remember that the
word you write should rhyme with the last word in the line
above.**

| crown | mouse | owl | clown |

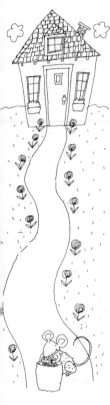

Who eats my cheese and lives in my house?

It's my friend, a little gray _____.

What do I hear that's a hoot, not a growl?

I hear the sound made by an _____.

Who do I see with a smile, not a frown?

I see a happy circus _____.

Where is the queen with hair so brown?

She's putting on her golden _____.

SCHOOL-HOME CONNECTION With your child,
play the game I Went to Town. Begin by saying,
"I went to town and saw a crowd." Your child
continues the game by repeating the sentence
and adding another word with the *ou* sound.

50

Extra Support
Banner Days

Name _____

▶ **Read each sentence. Circle and write the word that completes each sentence.**

1. _____ write a letter to you.

I'will
I'll
Iw'll

2. _____ get the letter soon.

You'll
You'will
Youll

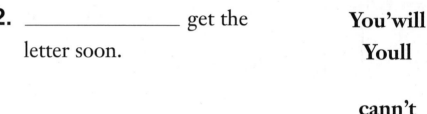

3. I _____ wait until you come for a visit.

cann't
can't
cant

4. _____ go fishing in the pond.

Well
Wew'll
We'll

5. _____ a great way to spend the day.

That's
Thats
That'is

6. _____ just one more week until you arrive!

Its
It'is
It's

SCHOOL-HOME CONNECTION Help your child write a letter to a friend. Have your child include at least three contractions in the letter.

51

Name _____

► **Read each sentence. Write the word that completes each sentence.**

isn't	I'll	don't	they'll	shouldn't	it's

1. _____ a good day to help someone.

2. My mom _____ work so hard.

3. _____ help with that!

4. I _____ mind washing the dishes.

5. _____ need some food.

6. _____ it fun to help out!

SCHOOL-HOME CONNECTION Talk about jobs that need to be done around the house. Discuss the importance of helping out. Have your child write two sentences about helping someone. Ask your child to use contractions.

53

Extra Support
Banner Days

▶ **Complete the sentences using Vocabulary Words.**

addresses	clerk	grown	honor	pour	route

1. A path you take every day

is a _____.

2. When you put juice into a glass, you

_____ the juice.

3. The person who works behind the counter

at a store is the _____.

4. _____ tell where people live.

5. When you get taller, you

have _____.

6. It is an _____
to win a prize.

TRY THIS! Write a paragraph about the type of job you would like to have someday. Use as many Vocabulary Words as you can. Draw a picture of what you might look like at work.

Choose the word that is the correct contraction for the underlined words.

Example I am

- ○ Iam
- ● I'm
- ○ Im

1 he is

- ○ hes
- ○ hee's
- ○ he's

> 💡 **Tip**
> Say the word aloud. Think about which sound is left out.

2 let us

- ○ lets
- ○ let's
- ○ letts

> 💡 **Tip**
> Remember that you are taking out letters, not adding them.

3 we will

- ○ we'll
- ○ well
- ○ w'ell

> 💡 **Tip**
> Remember that the apostrophe (') is placed where a letter was taken out.

Name _____

▶ **Read the paragraph. Then answer the questions.**

Today there are two ways to write and send a letter. The old way is to write a letter on paper. The new way is to write e–mail on a computer. To send a paper letter, you put it in an envelope with an address and a stamp. The post office takes your letter to the address. To send an e–mail, you press "send" and your e-mail goes to the other person's computer. For a paper letter, you have to buy a stamp. It does not cost anything to send e-mail. Both kinds of letters are ways to send a message to another person.

Name two ways e-mail and a letter written on paper are alike.

> **Tip**
> Reread the paragraph for details you may have missed.

1. _____

_____

2. _____

> **Tip**
> Things that are contrasted can usually be found close together.

3. Paper letters go through the _____, but e-mail goes from your computer

_____.

4. You have to buy _____ to send

paper letters, but _____ is free.

SCHOOL-HOME CONNECTION Gather some of your child's favorite toys. Ask your child to compare and contrast the toys.

57

Extra Support
Banner Days

▶ **Read the paragraph. Look at the underlined words. Make the underlined words mean more than one. Write the new words on the chart.**

Mr. and Mrs. Jones lived on a farm. They had two chickens, a hen, a cow, and a <u>calf</u>. The hen sat on her eggs all day long. Each spring they looked for the first green <u>leaf</u> to appear on the apple tree. In the fall, they made pies. The pies cooled on a wooden <u>shelf</u>. They gave <u>half</u> a pie to their neighbor. Mr. and Mrs. Jones had a very happy <u>life</u>.

1.	
2.	
3.	
4.	
5.	

SCHOOL-HOME CONNECTION With your child, make up new sentences using the words on this page. Try to make the sentences into a story.

58

Extra Support
Banner Days

Name _____

▶ **Write the letters *ew* or *ui* to complete each picture name.**

1. s _____ t

2. ch _____

3. st _____

4. dr _____

5. scr _____ s

6. fr _____ t

7. n _____ s

8. thr _____

9. j _____ ce

SCHOOL-HOME CONNECTION Talk with your child about different instruments that musicians play. Ask your child which instruments he or she likes best.

59

Extra Support
Banner Days

Name _____

▶ **Read the word. Circle the pictures whose names have the same vowel sounds.**

1. grew

  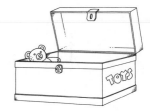

2. juice

JAIL

3. chew

▶ **Read the sentences. Write the word that best completes each one.**

4. The new _____ lined up.

recruits   rest   recipes

5. Peaches are my favorite _____.

flood   fruit   flew

6. He ran in _____ of the dog.

pursuit   present   purse

SCHOOL-HOME CONNECTION With your child, write two words with the *oo* sound that rhyme. Write a four-line poem using the two rhyming words.

61

Extra Support
Banner Days

▶ **On the line, write the Vocabulary Word to complete each sentence.**

appeared
imitated

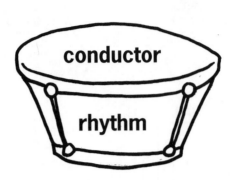
conductor
rhythm

created
startled

1. The girl beat the drum—boom–boom–boom. She beat a

   _____ on the drum.

2. We made a drum from a box. By doing this, we

   _____ a drum.

3. We were seen in a play. We _____ in a play.

4. Mr. Perez was the leader of our band. Mr. Perez was the

   _____ of our band.

5. We heard the sound of rain. We _____ the
   sound by tapping on a drum.

6. The loud drum surprised us. The loud drum

   _____ us.

TRY THIS! Write a few sentences about the type of music you enjoy the most. Use as many Vocabulary Words as you can.

Syllable Rule   Remember to divide the word after the consonant when it follows the *VC/V* pattern. Example: lem/on

▶ Write each word from the box, dividing it into syllables.

| civil | habit | level | model | robin |

fin/ish

1. _____

2. _____

3. _____

4. _____

5. _____

Extra Support
Banner Days

Name _____

▶ **Choose the meaning the underlined word has in the sentence.**

1 The school band got to the park early.

○ to stop a car in a place

○ an open place where people can play

Tip
Notice that *park* can be an action word (to stop–) and a naming word (a place–). In which way is the word used in the sentence?

2 The air was <u>still</u> chilly.

○ quiet

○ up to this time

Tip
Try saying the sentence to yourself by replacing *still* with each meaning. Which meaning makes more sense?

3 She drummed a fast <u>beat</u>.

○ a regular rhythm

○ to win instead of someone else

Tip
Think about what the common terms *drum beat* or *heart beat* mean.

SCHOOL-HOME CONNECTION With your child, make a list of words that have more than one meaning. Make up sentences with the different meanings. **65**

Extra Support
Banner Days

Name _____

▶ **Read the sentences. Circle the words that contain *oi* or *oy*.**

Who is Noisy?

1. A boy is wearing a cowboy hat.

2. The girl will use the coins to buy a box of blueberries.

3. A baby is holding a toy whale.

4. The man buys a bag of soil for his flowers.

5. The baby is making a lot of noise.

66

Extra Support
Banner Days

Name _____

▶ **Circle and write the word that completes the sentence.**

1. Did the big giraffe write

that _____?

paragraph
pine
pool

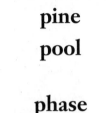

2. I took a _____ of
my sister's big toe.

phase
photo
pony

3. Here's a _____ I
made for math.

grape
grain
graph

4. Do you think this cotton puff is

soft or _____? .

rough
ring
rest

5. When she brushed the dust off,
I started

to _____.

carts
caught
cough

6. He put his hat on the little
calf, and everyone began

to _____.

laugh
long
learn

SCHOOL-HOME CONNECTION With your child, talk
about things that make him or her laugh. Encourage
your child to write sentences describing these things,
using as many *ph* and *gh* words as possible.

67

Extra Support
Banner Days

Name _____

▶ **Read the word. Circle the picture of another word that uses *ph* or *gh* letters to make the *f* sound.**

1. petrogylphs

2. paragraph

3. photo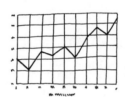

▶ **Read the sentences. Write the word that best completes each one.**

4. There is _____ popcorn for everyone.

      enough   enter   empty

5. The rope feels _____.

      route   rough   rowboat

6. The dust made him _____.

      court   count   cough

 SCHOOL-HOME CONNECTION With your child
make a list of words with the letters *ph* or *gh* that
make the *f* sound. Choose two words and write a
sentence for each word. Then have your child draw
pictures that tell about the sentences.

69

Extra Support
Banner Days

Name _____

▶ **Complete the sentences using the Vocabulary**
Words from the box.

| dappled | exhibition | landscape business |
| thousands | ranch | |

1. A pony with light and dark spots is a

_____ pony.

2. When you show or do something in front of a lot
of people, you are having an

_____ .

3. When you have more than hundreds, you have

_____ .

4. A _____ is a farm in the
country where horses, sheep, or cattle are raised.

5. A company that takes care of lawns, trees, plants, and

gardens is called a _____ .

 TRY THIS! Draw a picture of a ranch. Write three or four sentences about your picture. Use as many Vocabulary Words as you can.

▶ **Choose the word that has the same sound as the underlined letters in the first word.**

Example nep<u>h</u>ew

- ○ niece
- ● five
- ○ review

Tip

Be sure you know the sound the underlined letters make. If you are not sure about the sounds in one word, look down the page and find other words that you might know that have a **gh** or **ph** that make an **f** sound.

1 lau<u>gh</u>

- ○ crazy
- ○ phrase
- ○ gravy

2 tele<u>ph</u>one

- ○ river
- ○ listen
- ○ enough

Tip

Say the first word aloud and listen to the underlined letters. Then read each answer choice and listen for the same sound.

3 lau<u>gh</u>ing

- ○ elephant
- ○ lacking
- ○ going

Tip

Be sure to look for the sound in the underlined letters.

▶ **Read the story. Then answer the questions.**

Kit and Sunny

Kit had a horse named Sunny. Sunny was a beautiful black horse. It had a white star on its forehead. One day, Kit took Sunny out for a ride. When Kit rode past the town bank, she saw the robber, No Good Ned. He was running out with a sack of gold! Sunny and Kit chased the robber. Kit used her lasso to catch No Good Ned. Sunny and Kit saved the day!

1 Which sentence is important enough to put in a summary of this story?
Kit and Sunny caught a robber. *or* Kit's horse was black with a white star.

_____

_____

💡 Tip
Remember that a summary tells what a story is mostly about. Which sentence tells the most important thing that happens in this story?

2 Which sentence is ***not*** important enough to put in a summary of this story?
Kit used her lasso to catch the robber. *or* Sunny was a great horse.

_____

_____

💡 Tip
A summary tells only the most important events. Reread the story. Then read each answer choice.

SCHOOL-HOME CONNECTION Read a short story or newspaper article to your child. Ask your child to summarize and retell the story.

Extra Support
Banner Days

Name _____

▶ **Read the story. Circle all the words that have**
_oo_ or _ue_ and sound like glue. Write all of the
words on the chart. Write the words only once.

Goose liked the rain. He sat on the roof.

He waited for rain. One day at noon some

friends stopped at the barn. Goose heard

their voices. Then it started to rain.

Everyone put on their boots to play. "Can I

play too?" Goose asked. Goose took his blue

umbrella. Goose jumped in puddles until the

moon came up.

1.	
2.	
3.	
4.	
5.	
6.	
7.	

SCHOOL-HOME CONNECTION Ask your child
to name two words from the chart above that
rhyme. Work with your child to use the two words
in a short poem.

Extra Support
Banner Days

Name _____

▶ **Circle and write the word that completes the sentence.**

1. My grandmother lives above the grocery store in the _____ building on the block.

tall
taller
tallest

2. Paul runs _____ than Ming does.

fast
faster
fastest

3. I took the _____ cupcake on the shelf.

small
smaller
smallest

4. This bunch of flowers is _____ than that one.

fresh
fresher
freshest

5. My dog Bobo is the _____ dog in the world.

smart
smarter
smartest

SCHOOL-HOME CONNECTION With your child, compare Saturday morning activities with weekday morning activities. Have your child draw two pictures, one of a typical Saturday and one of a weekday. Help your child write sentences about each picture using words with –er and –est endings.

Extra Support
Banner Days

Name _____

► **Write the word that best completes each sentence.**

| happier | freshest | happiest | smallest | smarter | taller |

1. 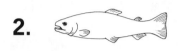 My grandfather is _____ than my grandmother.

2. 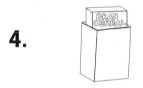 My mother picks the _____ fish at the market.

3.  For my dollhouse, my aunt gave me the _____ bowl she had.

4.  It is _____ to go shopping early in the morning than late in the afternoon.

5.  My family is _____ living in the city than in the country.

6. Chinese New Year is the _____ day of the year for me.

SCHOOL-HOME CONNECTION Talk about different types of neighborhoods or areas near your home. Help your child use words with –er and –est endings. Make separate lists of the words ending in –er and those ending in –est.

Extra Support
Banner Days

Name _____

▶ **Complete the sentences. Write a Vocabulary Word from the box on each line.**

| celebrations | develop | furious |
| graceful | grocery store | students |

1. You can buy food at a _____.

2. Children in school are _____.

3. If you are very angry, you are _____.

4. Parties and parades are kinds of _____.

5. When you move or do something in a beautiful way,

you are _____.

6. When you grow or change over time, you

_____.

TRY THIS! Draw a picture of you and a friend at a birthday party. Write about your picture. Use as many Vocabulary Words as you can.

Extra Support
Banner Days

Syllable Rule • **When a single consonant is between two vowels, divide before the consonant. Try the first syllable long. If the word makes sense, keep it!**

Example: ti/ger pa/per

▶ **Read the story. Look at the underlined words and write them where they belong in the chart below. Remember to divide the words into syllables.**

The houses in the big city are like huge columns that seem to touch the sky. The <u>major</u> library is so big that thousands of people can study there.  There's lots to do. I like to have <u>bagels</u> with cheese at a different <u>diner</u> every day. If I miss being in <u>nature</u>, I go to a special place in the middle of the city. It's the biggest park I ever saw. It has a forest and <u>tulip</u> gardens. Best of all, on <u>Fridays</u> I sit in the park and eat ice cream!

1. _____ 2. _____

3. _____ 4. _____

5. _____ 6. _____

▶ **Read the paragraph and answer the questions.**

Chinese restaurants are popular all over the United States. People like the many choices. You can get chicken, beef, pork, or seafood mixed with all kinds of vegetables. You can get vegetables and rice with no meat. You can get different sauces. Another thing people like about Chinese restaurants is the fast service. Most Chinese meals are cooked in a deep pan with rounded sides. The pan, called a wok, cooks food quickly and evenly.

1 Which sentence is an important detail that supports the main idea of the paragraph?

⬤ Tip
Find the main idea. It is often at the beginning of the paragraph. Then think about the details. Important details support the main idea.

○ You can get a meal with no meat at all.

○ You can get different sauces.

○ People like the many choices.

2 Which sentence is an important detail that supports the main idea of the paragraph?

⬤ Tip
The important details are often more general statements.

○ Another thing people like about Chinese take-out restaurants is the fast service.

○ Meals are cooked in a deep pan with rounded sides.

○ The pan, called a wok, cooks food quickly and evenly.

SCHOOL-HOME CONNECTION With your child, tell the story of an adventure you shared. Decide which details support the main idea.

81

Extra Support
Banner Days

▶ **Read the sentences. Circle the words that end in *-ful* or *-less*. Then write the word on the line.**

A Joyful Day

1. A beautiful rainbow is in the sky. _____

2. A harmless kitten is in the grass. _____

3. A cheerful bunny hops away. _____

4. The girl is careful not to get wet. _____

5. The birds are thankful for a sunny day. _____

SCHOOL-HOME CONNECTION Discuss with your child some things you are thankful for and some things that make you cheerful. Then have your child write two sentences using the words *thankful* and *cheerful*.

82

Extra Support
Banner Days

Name _____

▶ **Write the letters *air* or *are* to complete each picture name. Then trace the whole word.**

1. _____ port
2. _____ h
3. silverw _____

4. _____ ch
5. _____ p
6. _____ c

7. _____ sc
8. _____ sh
9. _____ squ

10. _____ planes
11. _____ st _____ s
12. _____ rep

SCHOOL-HOME CONNECTION With your child make
a list of *–air* and *–are* words. Ask your child to choose
two words and write a sentence for each. Then have
your child draw a picture to illustrate each sentence.

Extra Support
Banner Days

Name _____

▶ **Read each sentence. Write the word that completes each sentence.**

careful	dare	rare	chair	airport	pair

1.

The cat is sleeping on

the _____.

2.

It is _____ to find a
treasure chest in the park.

3.

Do you _____ to
dream about your future?

4.

I cannot find my _____
of mittens.

5.

My grandma and I went to the

_____.

6.

I am very _____ with my
grandmother's ring.

SCHOOL-HOME CONNECTION Ask your child
to think of words that rhyme with *chair*. Help make
a list of these rhyming words. Ask your child to
write the words with *air* in one column and the
words with *are* in another column.

85

Extra Support
Banner Days

▶ **On each line, write the Vocabulary Word from the box to solve the riddle.**

| flock | glide | harbor | soared | swooping |

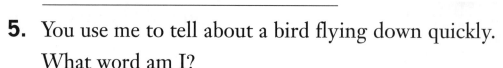

1. I am a place where ships come in.
   What am I?

   _____

2. When a plane flew high in the clouds,
   you used me to tell what the plane did.
   What word am I?

   _____

3. I am a group of animals.
   What am I?

   _____

4. I tell about moving easily.
   What am I?

   _____

5. You use me to tell about a bird flying down quickly.
   What word am I?

   _____

TRY THIS! Imagine that you are a bird flying high in the sky. Write about what you see. Use as many Vocabulary Words as you can in your sentences.

Extra Support
Banner Days

Name _____

Abuela

R–controlled
Vowels
Words with
air, are
TEST PREP

▶ **Choose the word that has the same sound as the underlined letters in the first word.**

Example h<u>ai</u>r

- ○ heart
- ● dare
- ○ rear

1 c<u>are</u>

- ○ car
- ○ ear
- ○ stair

> **Tip**
> Say each choice to yourself. Be sure each word makes sense when you say it.

2 <u>ai</u>rport

- ○ artist
- ○ part
- ○ shared

> **Tip**
> Ignore the choices that don't have the same sound.

3 squ<u>are</u>

- ○ fairground
- ○ school
- ○ quiet

> **Tip**
> Be sure you look for the sound in the underlined letters only.

▶ **Read the paragraph and answer the questions.**

Two men talked loudly. One man pointed at his watch and then looked at the door. He shook his head. Just then a third man walked through the door. The two men stopped talking and walked over to him. They pointed at their watches.

1. What do you think the two men are talking about?

_____

_____

2. How do you know this?

_____

_____

3. Is the third man late or on time?

_____

_____

4. How do you know this?

_____

_____

SCHOOL-HOME CONNECTION With your child, discuss common occurrences at home, such as making dinner and getting ready for school. Ask what signals help your child infer what is going on.

89

Extra Support
Banner Days

Name _____

▶ **Read the sentences. Circle the words that contain the suffixes –*ing* and –*ly*.**

A Day at the Park

1. A girl is standing in the sandbox.

2. The little boy is licking his ice cream cone carefully.

3. The man is drawing a picture.

4. A woman is planting flowers.

5. The birds are happily singing in the trees.

SCHOOL-HOME CONNECTION Talk with your child about what each of you likes to do when you visit a park. Discuss the activities that are illustrated above. Use words ending in –*ing* or –*ly*.

Extra Support
Banner Days

Name _____

▶ **Choose the word that names the picture.
Write the word on the line.**

1.

foot
fort
food

_____

2.

stood
stored
stone

_____

3.

bark
book
bag

_____

4.

would
wood
work

_____

5.

cord
cork
cook

_____

6.

hoop
howl
hook

_____

7.

look
load
lock

_____

8.

scoot
soot
soon

_____

SCHOOL-HOME CONNECTION Look out the
window with your child. Help your child write one
or two sentences about the view, using the pattern,
"When I look out the window, I see . . . ."

91

Name _____

▶ **Read the sentences.
Write the word
that best completes
each one.**

1. I wish I _____ visit
a place that is far away.   **could   can   cough**

2. I _____ see all
the wonderful sights.   **wood   would   wound**

3. The new things might

_____ strange to me.   **load   look   luck**

4. It is _____ to
see new places.   **good   goat   got**

5. I will visit my father's

_____

friend in India.   **building   boyhood   boyish**

6. I read a _____
about India.   **boat   buck   book**

7. Dad says that I _____
finish my homework
before I go.   **shell   should   shall**

SCHOOL-HOME CONNECTION Have your child
draw a picture of a place he or she would like to visit.
Ask your child to write a sentence at the top of the
picture, using the sentence pattern, "I would like to
go to . . . ."

Extra Support
Banner Days

▶ **Complete the sentences. Write a word from
the box on each line.**

connects	distance	features	mapmaker	peel

1. _____ is the amount of space between two
places.

2. A _____ is a person who makes maps.

3. A bridge _____ two pieces of land.

4. _____ are parts of a large object.

5. When you pull the skin off of an orange, you

_____ the orange.

TRY THIS! Write three sentences about a place you have visited. Was it
far away? Did you enjoy yourself? Use as many Vocabulary
Words as you can.

Name _____

▶ **Read the word in the box. Write it under the correct column. Write the words in syllables**

squirrel	butcher	princess	children
trumpet	hundred	basket	daughter
	slipper	sandwich	

VCCCV Words

1. _____

2. _____

3. _____

4. _____

5. _____

VCCV Words

6. _____

7. _____

8. _____

9. _____

10. _____

SCHOOL-HOME CONNECTION Help your child create a list of words with the VCCCV or VCCV syllable pattern. Then ask your child to tell you the number of syllables in each word.

96

Extra Support
Banner Days

Name _____

▶ **Read the Table of Contents. Then answer the questions.**

The Best Bug Book
Table of Contents

Chapter 1   *Big Bugs*   Page 1
Chapter 2   *Little Bugs*   Page 5
Chapter 3   *How to Feed a Bug*   Page 10
Chapter 4   *How to Build a Bug House*   Page 15
Chapter 5   *How to Keep Bugs Without Scaring Your Mom*   Page 20

1 On which page would you begin to find information on feeding bugs?

○ Page 1

○ Page 5

○ Page 10

○ Page 15

💡 **Tip**

Read each chapter title. Look for the chapter about how to feed a bug. Then look across to see on which page that chapter starts.

2 Which chapter would tell you the most about big bugs?

○ Chapter 1

○ Chapter 2

○ Chapter 3

○ Chapter 4

💡 **Tip**

Look for the chapter about big bugs.

SCHOOL-HOME CONNECTION With your child, look at a table of contents. Have your child try to figure out what kind of information might be in the various chapters.

Extra Support
Banner Days

▶ **Read the story. Circle all the words that begin
with *re-* and *pre-*. Then write all of the words
on the chart.**

Did you hear about the moose who went to preschool?
First he packed his backpack, but then he repacked it. He
knocked over a block tower and had to rebuild it. His
lunch was cold and he asked his teacher to reheat it. He
learned to recycle his old paper. The moose had fun. He
decided to return the next day.

1.
2.
3.
4.
5.
6.

SCHOOL-HOME CONNECTION With your child
make up a story about an animal that visits your
child's classroom. What would the animal do all day?
Would the animal learn anything? Ask your child to use
words with the prefixes *pre* and *re*.

98

Extra Support
Banner Days

Name _____

▶ **Circle and write the word that completes each sentence.**

1. Will Sam sip the _____?

          soup   soap   sap

2. Does Wanda's _____ hurt?

          wood   wound   wall

3. Will you drive _____ the tunnel?

          throughout   throughway   through

4. You should join our _____.

          goop   group   good

5. This _____ is the quickest way to get there.

          through   throughout   throughway

6. Use this _____ to save a dollar!

          coop   couple   coupon

SCHOOL-HOME CONNECTION Help your child make up a recipe for a crazy soup. Write down the name of the soup and the ingredients.

99

Extra Support
Banner Days

Name _____

▶ **Write the word that completes each sentence.**

| soup | youth | throughout | routine | you | through |

1. Bob and Ray travel

_____ the country.

2. They follow the same

_____ every day.

3. They always have

_____ for lunch.

4. They drive _____
many states.

5. They spend the night

at _____ centers.

6. Would _____ like
to go with them sometime?

SCHOOL-HOME CONNECTION With your child,
look at a map. Draw a route from your hometown to
a place where a friend or relative lives. Show your
child which places you would have to drive through to
get there.

101

Extra Support
Banner Days

▶ **Connect the Vocabulary Words in the suitcases to their meanings.**

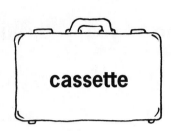

cassette

1. friends

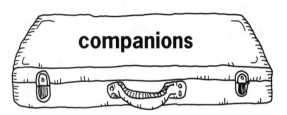

companions

2. strong

luggage

3. a music tape

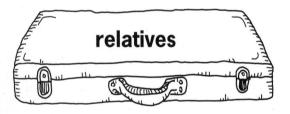

relatives

4. bags

5. people related to each other

sturdy

 TRY THIS! Write a paragraph about a trip you have taken. Use as many Vocabulary Words as you can.

Name _____

▶ **Choose the word that has the same sound as the underlined letters in the first word.**

Example s<u>ou</u>p

- ○ train
- ○ crow
- ● through

1 y<u>ou</u>

- ○ brook
- ○ young
- ○ soup

Tip

Say each choice aloud and listen for the underlined sound.

2 tr<u>ou</u>p

- ○ throughway
- ○ trust
- ○ throw

Tip

Ignore the choices that don't make sense.

3 thr<u>ou</u>ghout

- ○ throwing
- ○ regroup
- ○ outgrow

Tip

Remember the two different spellings of the sound.

▶ **Read each paragraph. Then answer the questions.**

Puerto Rico is the best place for your vacation. You will love the sunshine and our beautiful beaches. Great food and friendly people make your visit special. In the evenings, you will want to dance all night to the wonderful music in our clubs. Bring your children and have a vacation you will always remember.

1 What is the author's purpose—
to entertain *or* to persuade?

💡 **Tip**
Think about the words the author uses to describe Puerto Rico. How does the author make Puerto Rico sound?

_____

2 What does the author want you to do—come to Puerto Rico *or* take a cruise?

💡 **Tip**
Think about the subject of the paragraph.

_____

SCHOOL-HOME CONNECTION With your child, look at an advertisement or newspaper article. Discuss with your child the author's purpose for writing the item .

105

Extra Support
Banner Days

Name _____

▶ **Read the story. Circle all the words with *mis–* or *under–*. Write all the words on the chart.**

Mole and Beaver are going to undertake a big job. "Be sure you understand what we have to do," said Mole. "You work underground and I'll work underwater," said Beaver. "We'll write it down so we don't misunderstand," said Mole. "Don't misspell any words," said Beaver. "Let's go," they said. "Where's our note?" asked Beaver. "I misplaced it," said Mole.

1.	
2.	
3.	
4.	
5.	
6.	
7.	

SCHOOL-HOME CONNECTION Write the words from this exercise on a sheet of paper. Ask your child to highlight or underline the *mis* or *under* in each word. Then have your child write two sentences—one with a *mis–* word and one with an *under–* word.

106

Extra Support
Banner Days

Name _____

▶ **Choose the word that names the picture. Write the word on the line.**

1.
called
crawled
cold

_____

2.
you'll
you
yawn

_____

3.
pat
paw
put

_____

4.
seesaw
season
selling

_____

5.
say
saw
sew

_____

6.
jail
jaw
jelly

_____

7.
last
lane
lawn

_____

8.
dangle
daughter
dagger

_____

9.
call
cast
caught

_____

10.
natural
naughty
nothing

_____

11.
saw
stew
straw

_____

12.
claw
call
cause

_____

SCHOOL-HOME CONNECTION With your child make up nonsense sentences using as many of the *au* and *aw* words as possible. For example: "The naughty lawn crawled on to the seesaw." Encourage your child to play with the sounds.

Extra Support
Banner Days

Name _____

▶ **Write the words from the box that name the
pictures. Then write a word that rhymes with
the other words. Draw a picture for it.**

yawn	draw	fought
taught	paw	dawn

1. _____   _____   _____

2. _____   _____   _____

3. _____   _____   _____

SCHOOL-HOME CONNECTION Help your child
make up a story about sailing. Try to use as many
aw or au words as you can.

109

Extra Support
Banner Days

Name _____

▶ On the line, write the Vocabulary Word to complete the caption for each picture.

| cozy | drifted | fleet | launched | looming | realized |

1. The shadow was _____ over the dog.

2. Marco _____ it was raining when he went outside.

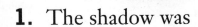

3. A _____ of ships sailed by.

4. Pedro _____ the toy rocket.

5. I was in my _____ bed.

6. My boat _____ on the pond.

TRY THIS! There are many different ways to travel—by boat, airplane, train, car, and bicycle. Write a few sentences about your favorite way to travel. Use as many Vocabulary Words as you can.

Name _____

Syllable Rule • **When two vowels come together in a word and have separate sounds, divide the word between the two vowels.**
Example: gi/ant

• **When a single consonant is between two vowels, divide before the consonant. Try the first syllable long. If the word makes sense, keep it!**
Example: ti/ger

• **If the word does not make sense, divide after the consonant and try it short.**
Example: lem/on

▶ Read the words in the box. Write each word where it belongs in the chart. Divide the words into syllables.

basin	divide	seven	molar	create
neon	poet	item	water	

di/ner	flu/id	nev/er
1. _____	4. _____	7. _____
2. _____	5. _____	8. _____
3. _____	6. _____	9. _____

Name _____

▶ **Choose the correct word to complete each sentence.**

1 Please _____ me a letter when you take your boat trip.

- ○ right
- ○ write

Tip

Homophones are words that sound alike, but they have different meanings. Choose the word that makes most sense.

2 The mouse's home was flooded by _____.

- ○ rein
- ○ rain

3 Three mice and one mole made _____ small animals on the ship.

- ○ four
- ○ for

Tip

Try to picture the right answer in your mind. (Hint: How do you write the number 4?)

SCHOOL-HOME CONNECTION With your child, make a list of a few homophones. Help your child draw a picture showing the various meanings of the words.

113

Extra Support
Banner Days

Name _____

▶ **Read the sentences. Circle the words that are contractions. Then write the contraction on the lines.**

It's a Parade!

1. Isn't the parade wonderful? _____

2. The boy with the flag can't see the parade.

_____

3. You'll soon see the elephant. _____

4. You shouldn't miss the funny clowns. _____

5. I'll wave to the man riding on the elephant! _____

SCHOOL-HOME CONNECTION Have your child draw a scene from a parade and then write two sentences telling about it. Encourage your child to use at least one word that is a contraction.

114

Extra Support
Banner Days

Name _____

▶ **Write the word from the box that rhymes with the underlined word part.**

leave	pure	bend	bold	hair
cord	bed	flight	blue	blow

1. over<u>due</u> _____

2. over<u>night</u> _____

3. over<u>board</u> _____

4. over<u>flow</u> _____

5. over<u>head</u> _____

6. un<u>friend</u>ly _____

7. un<u>sure</u> _____

8. un<u>eve</u>n _____

9. un<u>fair</u> _____

10. un<u>fold</u> _____

LATE

SCHOOL-HOME CONNECTION With your child make lists of words that rhyme with *fair, head, fold,* and *friend*.

115

Extra Support
Banner Days

Name _____

▶ **Add *un* or *over* to the words in the box to finish the sentences.**

due	flow	night	fair
tie	lock	friendly	head

1. The mean dog was _____.

2. An airplane flew _____.

3. I used my key to _____ the door.

4. My library book was late.

It was _____.

5. The bow on my present was

hard to _____.

6. That rule is _____!

7. John slept _____
at his grandma's house.

8. A river can _____
its banks in a storm.

SCHOOL-HOME CONNECTION Make a list of
words that can have either *over* or *un* added to
them. Then ask your child to tell you which prefix
should go with each word.

Extra Support
Banner Days

▶ **Write the correct Vocabulary Word on the line to solve each riddle.**

feat	heroine	hospitality
refused	spectators	stood

1. I am a girl who does brave things. Who am I ?

_____

2. I am something that people do with great strength or courage.

What word am I? _____

3. We watch interesting events. Who are we?

_____

4. When you said "No!" you did this. What did you do?

_____

5. I mean the nice treatment of guests. What word am I?

_____

6. You did this when you got up from a chair. What did you do?

_____

 TRY THIS! Write a paragraph about someone you think is a hero or heroine. Use as many Vocabulary Words as you can.

| **Syllable Rule** | • **Divide a compound word between the two words:** *shoe/lace*. |

• **Divide between the base word and the prefix, the suffix, or ending:** *pre/view*.

• **Divide between two consonants that fall between two vowels:** *ham/mer*.

▶ **Read the words. Write each word in syllables.**

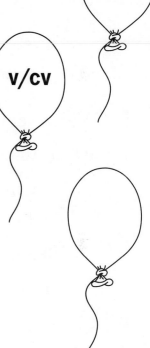

vc/cv

v/cv

1. dollar _____

2. piglet _____

3. pollen _____

4. cowboy _____

5. fearful _____

6. helpless _____

7. Sunday _____

8. problem _____

▶ **Read the story. Then answer the questions.**

The weather was terrible. Heavy snow was falling in the city. The ground was very icy. Linda, the pilot, looked at the dark sky. This kind of weather could be very dangerous. The safety of the passengers was most important. She knew what she had to do. She could not fly the plane now.

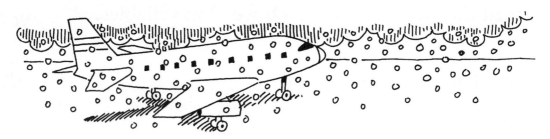

1 Which sentence would go best at the end of the paragraph?

○ She must wait until the bad weather passed.

○ She must clean the airplane's cockpit.

○ She must fix the airplane's wings.

> 💡 **Tip**
> Read the paragraph with each possible sentence at the end. Choose the one that sounds the best.

2 When the bad weather passes, the first thing Linda will probably do is

○ get on another airplane.

○ fly the plane.

○ land the airplane.

> 💡 **Tip**
> Think about why Linda is not flying the plane.

SCHOOL-HOME CONNECTION Read a story to your child that he or she has never heard. Have your child guess the ending before you read it.

121

Extra Support
Banner Days

Name _____

Ruth Law Thrills a
Nation

Review:
Vowel Digraphs:
/oo// ew, ui

▶ **Write the words from the box that best
complete the poem. Remember that the word
you write should rhyme with the last word in the line above.**

pursuit	fruit	new	chew

My pony Sprite is very cute.

He always eats a lot

of _____.

He'll eat an apple, sometimes two.

He likes to stand around

and _____

If a bandit steals some loot,

Sprite will run in hot _____.

When I'm with Sprite I always do

Something fun and

something _____.

 SCHOOL-HOME CONNECTION Ask your child
to think of words that rhyme with *new* and *juice.*
Help your child make a list. Then have him or her
circle the words with the letters *ew* or *ui.*

122

Extra Support
Banner Days

Page 1
Written word:
1. hide
2. ride
3. slide
4. hid
5. inside
6. wide

Circled word:
1. hide
2. ride
3. slide
4. hid
5. inside
6. wide

Page 3
1. picture of slide
2. picture of jar lid
3. picture of child on bike
4. wide
5. kid
6. eyelid

Page 4
1. not shiny
2. very interesting
3. very good-looking
4. almost not
5. to the left or to the right
6. shining or glittering
7. saw

Page 6
1. 1
2. 3
3. 2
4. 2
5. 2
6. 1
7. 2

8. 2
9. 3

Page 7
1. Third circle
2. Second circle

Page 8
1. Third circle
2. Third circle
3. Third circle

Page 9
1. slide
2. inside
3. did
4. ride

Page 10
1. snake
2. name
3. same
4. make
5. mistake
6. brake
7. flame
8. games

Page 12
1. same
2. games
3. name
4. make
5. snake
6. take

Page 13
1. homework
2. minutes
3. treat
4. always
5. snuggle

Page 15
1. Third circle
2. First circle
3. Second circle
4. Third circle

Page 16
Responses may vary.

Page 17
1. hide
2. slide
3. ride
4. eyelid
5. inside

Page 18
1. barked
2. opened
3. licked
4. thanked
5. painted
6. backed
7. mailed
8. checked

Page 20
1. remarked
2. opened
3. checked
4. barked
5. thanked
6. licked

Page 21
1. woods
2. sniffing
3. chipmunks
4. picked
5. south

Page 23
1. Second circle
2. First circle
3. Second circle

Page 24
1. on a farm
2. in the summer

Page 25
1. snake
2. name
3. games
4. make
5. became
6. mistake
7. take

Page 26
1. studied
2. cried
3. carried
4. checked
5. copied
6. called
7. hurried
8. walked
9. jumped
10. boiled
11. fried
12. married

Page 28
1. Picture of bride and groom
2. Picture of boy crying
3. Picture of egg frying
4. studied
5. hurried
6. copied

Page 29
1. by yourself
2. to make happy
3. very good
4. a field
5. why something happens
6. ruined

Page 31
1. acted
2. toasted
3. blended
4. hunted
5. folded
6. two
7. two
8. one
9. two
10. one

Page 32
1. Fourth circle
2. Third circle

Page 33
1. painted
2. mailed
3. backed
4. opened
5. barked
6. licked
7. thanked
8. remarked

Page 34
1. gate
2. acrobat
3. cat
4. plate
5. state
6. create
7. sat
8. appreciate

Page 36
1. bat; cat
2. plate; skate
3. gate; state
4. flat
5. create
6. acrobat

Page 37
1. gathered
2. raced
3. clustered
4. wandered
5. amazing

Page 39
1. broad / cast
2. book / stores
3. pin / point
4. day / dream
5. dog / house

Page 40
1. nervous
2. proud
3. in the classroom

Page 41
1. studied
2. fried
3. cried
4. tried
5. hurried
6. worried
7. replied
8. carried

Page 42
1. clock
2. pack
3. rocket
4. crack
5. flock
6. lock
7. horseback
8. dock
9. snack
10. black
11. shock
12. track

Page 44
1. crack; pack; Accept reasonable responses.
2. lock; flock; Accept reasonable responses.
3. locket; pocket; Accept reasonable responses.

Page 45
1. granddaughter
2. grew
3. enormous
4. planted
5. turnip
6. strong

Page 47
1. ar / row
2. bar / rel
3. bot / tom
4. com / ma
5. fol / low
6. hap / pen
7. mir / ror
8. piz / za
9. traf / fic
10. yel / low

Page 48
1. First circle
2. Third circle

Page 49
2. cat
4. garden
6. lamp
8. soil
10. vegetable

Page 50
1. hat
2. crate
3. fat
4. skate

Page 51
1. Earth
2. pear
3. earn
4. pearl
5. learn
6. search
7. heart
8. early
9. rehearse

Page 53
1. heard
2. yearned
3. researched
4. early
5. learned
6. rehearsed

Page 54
1. next to
2. jobs to do
3. a machine that makes a car move
4. not hard to do
5. to start to grow
6. something you use when you work

Page 56
1. v el / vet
2. mar / ket
3. tur / nip
4. win / dow
5. hal / ter
6. doc / tor
7. gar / den
8. mon / key
9. for / ward
10. win / ter

Page 57
1. Third circle
2. Second circle

Page 58
1. horseback
2. crack
3. rocket
4. flock

Page 59
1. Dr.
2. St.
3. Aug.
4. Wed.
5. Mr.

Page 61
1. Mrs.
2. Jan.
3. Tues.
4. Dr.
5. St.
6. Mr.

Page 62
1. promise
2. directions
3. cranes
4. twitch
5. worry

Page 64
1. First circle
2. Third circle
3. Third circle

Page 65
1. She will go to the circus.
2. Yes
3. She put on flying clothes.

Page 66
1. yearned
2. heard
3. research
4. learned
5. earned
6. rehearsed

Page 67
1. four
2. court
3. poured
4. course
5. fourteen

Page 69
1. fourth
2. resource
3. four
4. mourn
5. source
6. poured

Page 70
1. recipe
2. batter
3. smeared
4. buttery
5. yellow cake
6. perfect

Page 72
1. ham / mers
2. ham / mered
3. ques / tions
4. ques / tioned
5. but / tons
6. but / toned
7. won / ders
8. won / dered

Page 73
1. Second circle
2. Fourth circle
3. Third circle

Page 74
1. Third circle
2. Second circle

Page 75
1. Dr.
2. St.
3. Tues.
4. Aug.
5. Sun.
6. Dec.
7. Jan.
8. Wed.
9. Mr.

Page 76
1. star
2. farm
3. car
4. jar
5. park
6. arm
7. bark
8. charm
9. alarm

Page 78
1. bar; jar / Responses will vary.
2. alarm; charm / Responses will vary.
3. dark; park / Responses will vary.

Page 79
1. build it again
2. sad
3. part of the club
4. come late
5. everyone

Page 81
1. First circle
2. Third circle
3. First circle

Page 82
1. worked
2. earned
3. went to the museum

Page 83
1. Third circle
2. Second circle
3. Second circle

Page 84
1. four
2. court
3. source
4. fourteen
5. course
6. poured

Page 85
1. hear
2. year
3. beard
4. steer
5. cheers
6. nearby

Page 87
1. pioneer
2. clearing
3. nearby
4. reindeer
5. years
6. steer

Page 88
1. frontier
2. orchards
3. nearby
4. wild
5. tame
6. survive

Page 90
1. First circle
2. Second circle
3. First circle

Page 91
1. Fourth circle
2. First circle

Page 92
1. star
2. charm
3. far
4. dark

Page 93
1. string
2. strong
3. strap
4. three
5. throat
6. thread
7. sprout
8. ostrich
9. spray
10. stream
11. throne
12. stroller

Page 95
1. thread
2. spray
3. ostrich
4. sprout
5. stream
6. throat

Page 96
1. beautiful
2. ripens
3. nutrition
4. streams
5. protects

Page 98
1. riv / er
2. trav / el
3. po / lar
4. pal / ace
5. bro / ken
6. ho / tel
7. wag / on

8. free / zer
9. to / ken
10. ev / er

Page 99
1. Third circle
2. Second circle

Page 100
1. beard
2. year
3. clearing
4. nearby
5. pioneer
6. cheers
7. hear

Page 101
1. scooter
2. roof
3. food
4. boot
5. balloon
6. hoop
7. spoon
8. roots
9. broom
10. moon
11. room
12. tools

Page 103
1. cartoon
2. boots
3. scooter
4. smooth
5. roots
6. food

Page 104
1. forecast
2. discover
3. energy
4. source
5. shed

Page 106
1. a / ble
2. fa / ble
3. i / dle
4. ti / tle
5. bab / ble
6. can / dle
7. rat / tle
8. un / cle

Page 107
1. Second circle
2. Fourth circle

Page 108
1. springtime; sprout
2. sprays
3. through
4. streams
5. ostriches

Page 109
1. knock
2. gnat
3. writer
4. pocketknife
5. wrist
6. knot
7. write
8. knight
9. knit
10. sign
11. knee

Page 111
1. knight
2. gnat
3. wrist
4. sign
5. unknown
6. wrist

Page 112
1. knelt
2. beneath
3. wrinkled
4. shimmered
5. relay race
6. snug

Page 114
1. spar/kled
2. gig/gled
3. tan/gled
4. cir/cled
5. wrin/kled

Page 115
1. Fourth circle
2. Second circle

Page 116
1. early
2. earth
3. heard
4. searched
5. learn
6. pearl
7. earned

Page 117
1. cries
2. skies
3. copies
4. hobbies
5. beauties
6. cities

Page 119
1. hobbies
2. pennies
3. duties
4. studies
5. babies
6. cries

Page 120

1. bragged about something
2. walked very quietly
3. a covering worn on a king's head
4. a very small town
5. plants with long, thin stems

Page 122

1. Third circle
2. Second circle
3. First circle

Page 123

Responses may vary.

Page 124

1. source
2. Four
3. poured
4. Fourteen
5. course

Answer Key Volume 2 "Banner Days"

Page 1
1. mouth
2. brow
3. out
4. clown
5. sound
6. cow
7. crown
8. around
9. gown
10. house
11. frown
12. found

Page 3
1. house
2. How
3. around
4. Now
5. without
6. found

Page 4
1. boring
2. ducked
3. tractor
4. suppose
5. sense

Page 6
1. loud / ly
2. tak / ing
3. fear / less
4. care / ful
5. nic / est

Page 7
1. it was a rainy day.
2. it was time for arts and crafts.

Page 8
1. joyful
2. hairless
3. restful
4. mouthful
5. harmful
6. starless
7. cloudless
8. lifeless

Page 9
1. scooter
2. school
3. smooth
4. roots
5. moon
6. food
7. spoon
8. room
9. broom

Page 10
1. cowboys
2. joy
3. coin
4. oil
5. voices
6. point

Page 12
1. picture of boy
2. picture of coins
3. picture of toys
4. soil
5. oil
6. enjoyment

Page 13
1. captured
2. manners
3. imagination
4. Plains
5. vacation
6. matador
7. relax

Page 15
1. boy
2. point
3. destroy

Page 16
Possible responses given.
Cause: It rained.
Effect: The narrator washed the dog with toothpaste.
The narrator gave the dog a bath with human shampoo.

Page 17
1. reindeer
2. clearing
3. deer
4. nearby
5. year
6. beards
7. hear
8. cheers

Page 18
1. glue
2. moon
3. blue
4. noon
5. roof
6. pool
7. room
8. zoo
9. spoon
10. tool
11. boot
12. moose

Page 20
1. due
2. noon
3. true
4. too
5. clue
6. soon

Page 21
1. small pieces of information
2. to let down
3. very strongly
4. facts or knowledge
5. large bodies of salt water
6. to pet or rub

Page 23
1. head / band
2. back / pack
3. book / store
4. black / board
5. health / care
6. foot / ball
7. base / ball
8. when / ever
9. any / thing
10–12. Responses will vary.

Page 24
1. Fourth circle
2. Second circle

Page 25
1. knock
2. gnat
3. write
4. pocketknife

Page 26
1. shelf
2. leaf
3. shelves
4. calf
5. halves
6. elves
7. wives
8. leaves
9. wife
10. elf
11. half
12. calves

Page 28

1. life
2. leaves
3. leaf
4. half
5. halves
6. lives

Page 29

1. mimicked
2. fussed
3. pale
4. admired
5. notice
6. haze

Page 31

1. birth / day
2. cat / fish
3. horse / shoe
4. broad / cast
5. day / dream
6. pin / point
7. rain / bow
8. foot / step
9. side / walk
10. sun / shine
11. moon / light
12. key / hole

Page 32

1. sad
2. dark

Page 33

1. Sun.
2. Tues.
3. Wed.
4. Dr.
5. Jan.
6. Mr.
7. Aug.

Page 34

1. swimming
2. eating
3. completely
4. actually
5. starting
6. slowly

Page 36

1. doing
2. pouring
3. freezing
4. taking
5. standing
6. completely

Page 37

1. slippery
2. miserable
3. hatch
4. flippers
5. waddled
6. horizon

Page 39

1. extremely
2. running
3. tracing

Page 40

1. *All About Eggs* and *Bird Watching*
2. *Bird Tales*

Page 41

1. babies
2. cities
3. pennies
4. cookies
5. beauties
6. hobbies

Page 42

1. remove
2. preschool

Extra Support
Answer Key

3. replace
4. preview
5. prefix
6. recall

Page 44
1. preheat
2. return
3. repack
4. retie
5. prepay
6. recycle

Page 45
1. Objects
2. caused
3. removes
4. confused
5. typical
6. clasp
7. cornered

Page 47
1. pre / view
2. re / visit
3. un / fair
4. re / read
5. un / tie

Page 48
1. Fourth circle
2. Third circle

Page 49
1. misplaced
2. underbrush
3. mistook
4. underline
5. underdog
6. underfed

Page 50
1. mouse
2. owl
3. clown
4. crown

Page 51
1. I'll
2. You'll
3. can't
4. We'll
5. That's
6. It's

Page 53
1. It's
2. shouldn't
3. I'll
4. don't
5. They'll
6. Isn't

Page 54
1. route
2. pour
3. clerk
4. Addresses
5. grown
6. honor

Page 56
1. he's
2. let's
3. we'll

Page 57
Possible responses are given.
1. Both are ways to send a message to another person.
2. Both are written messages.
3. post office; to another computer.
4. stamps; e-mail

Page 58
1. calves
2. leaves
3. shelves
4. halves
5. lives

Page 59

1. suit
2. chew
3. stew
4. drew
5. screw
6. fruit
7. news
8. threw
9. juice

Page 61

1. picture of a newspaper
2. picture of a suit
3. picture of a screw
4. recruits
5. fruit
6. pursuit

Page 62

1. rhythm
2. created
3. appeared
4. conductor
5. imitated
6. startled

Page 64

1. civ / il
2. hab / it
3. lev / el
4. mod / el
5. rob / in

Page 65

1. Second circle
2. Second circle
3. First circle

Page 66

1. boy; cowboy
2. coins
3. toy
4. soil
5. noise

Page 67

1. paragraph
2. photo
3. graph
4. rough
5. cough
6. laugh

Page 69

1. picture of a laugh
2. picture of a telephone
3. picture of a graph
4. enough
5. rough
6. cough

Page 70

1. dappled
2. exhibition
3. thousands
4. ranch
5. landscape business

Page 72

1. phrase
2. enough
3. elephant

Page 73

1. Kit and Sunny caught a robber.
2. Sunny was a great horse.

Page 74

1. Goose
2. roof
3. noon
4. boots
5. too
6. blue
7. moon

Page 75

1. tallest
2. faster
3. smallest
4. fresher
5. smartest

Page 77
1. taller
2. freshest
3. smallest
4. smarter
5. happier
6. happiest

Page 78
1. grocery store
2. students
3. furious
4. celebrations
5. graceful
6. develop

Page 80
1. ma / jor
2. ba / gels
3. di / ner
4. na / ture
5. tu / lip
6. Fri / days

Page 81
1. Third circle
2. First circle

Page 82
1. beautiful
2. harmless
3. cheerful
4. careful
5. thankful

Page 83
1. airport
2. hair
3. silverware
4. chair
5. pair
6. care
7. scare
8. share
9. square
10. airplanes

11. stairs
12. repair

Page 85
1. chair
2. rare
3. dare
4. pair
5. airport
6. careful

Page 86
1. harbor
2. soared
3. flock
4. glide
5. swooping

Page 88
1. stair
2. shared
3. fairground

Page 89
Possible responses are given.
1. They are talking about the third man.
2. They stop talking and walk over to the man.
3. late
4. The two men point to their watches.

Page 90
1. standing
2. licking; carefully
3. drawing
4. planting
5. happily; singing

Page 91
1. foot
2. stood
3. book
4. wood
5. cook
6. hook
7. look
8. soot

Page 93
1. could
2. would
3. look
4. good
5. boyhood
6. book
7. should

Page 94
1. Distance
2. mapmaker
3. connects
4. Features
5. peel

Page 96
1. but / cher
2. chil / dren
3. hun / dred
4. daugh / ter
5. sand / wich
6. bas / ket
7. slip / per
8. prin / cess
9. trum / pet
10. squir / rel

Page 97
1. Page 10
2. Chapter 1

Page 98
1. preschool
2. repacked
3. rebuild
4. reheat
5. recycle
6. return

Page 99
1. soup
2. wound
3. through
4. group
5. throughway
6. coupon

Page 101
1. throughout
2. routine
3. soup
4. through
5. youth
6. you

Page 102
1. companions
2. sturdy
3. cassette
4. luggage
5. relatives

Page 104
1. soup
2. throughway
3. regroup

Page 105
Possible responses are given.
1. to persuade
2. Come to Puerto Rico.

Page 106
1. undertake
2. understand
3. underground
4. underwater
5. misunderstand
6. misspell
7. misplaced

Page 107
1. crawled
2. yawn
3. paw
4. seesaw
5. saw
6. jaw
7. lawn
8. daughter
9. caught
10. naughty
11. straw
12. claw

Page 109
1. fought; taught; Responses will vary.
2. paw; draw; Responses will vary.
3. dawn; yawn; Responses will vary.

Page 110
1. looming
2. realized
3. fleet
4. launched
5. cozy
6. drifted

Page 112
1. ba / sin
2. i / tem
3. mo / lar
4. cre / ate
5. ne / on
6. po / et
7. wa / ter
8. div / ide
9. sev / en

Page 113
1. write
2. rain
3. four

Page 114
1. Isn't
2. can't
3. You'll
4. shouldn't
5. I'll

Page 115
1. blue
2. flight
3. cord
4. blow
5. bed
6. bend
7. pure
8. leave
9. hair
10. bold

Page 117
1. unfriendly
2. overhead
3. unlock
4. overdue
5. untie
6. unfair
7. overnight
8. overflow

Page 118
1. heroine
2. feat
3. spectators
4. refused
5. hospitality
6. stood

Page 120
1. dol / lar
2. pig / let
3. pol / len
4. cow / boy
5. fear / ful
6. help / less
7. Sun / day
8. prob / lem

Page 121
1. First circle
2. Second circle

Page 122
1. fruit
2. chew
3. pursuit
4. new

Extra Support
Answer Key